Bath In

Bath In Quotes

*A Literary View From
Saxon Times Onwards*

Edited by
PAUL CRESSWELL

ASHGROVE PRESS, BATH

First published in Great Britain by
ASHGROVE PRESS LIMITED
26 Gay Street, Bath, Avon BA1 2PD

First published 1985

ISBN 0 906798 50 7

Photoset in 10½ point Goudy Oldstyle by
David Siddall & Associates
Bath

Printed & bound by Biddles Ltd
Guildford & Kings Lynn

To Vera

ACKNOWLEDGEMENTS

The editor and the publisher wish to thank the following for granting permission to quote from their various works: John Murray for *The Newest Bath Guide* by John Betjeman; Methuen for *In Search Of England* by H.V. Morton; A.P. Watt Ltd. for *Generally Speaking* by G.K. Chesterton, with the kind permission of Miss D.E. Collins; Jan Morris for *Bath, The Grand Old Spa*; Ian Burton for 'Liberty of the Clink'; the *Listener* for 'Reflections on a City' and 'Frank Lloyd Wright' by Alistair Cooke.

The cover picture 'View of Bath c. 1752' by Thomas Robbins is reproduced by courtesy of the British Museum

CONTENTS

ILLUSTRATIONS

INTRODUCTION

Bath has been my home now for a good many years and I cannot really imagine living anywhere else. I am guilty of taking much of Bath's formal eighteenth century splendour and cosy elegance for granted, behaving as a selfish lover might behave towards his mistress, never managing to return her favours. This book, which I began four years ago, is my way of saying thank you to Bath and so making good that fault. Actually the idea for the book arose co-incidentally with the completion of an L.P. record *The Humours of Bath* which I co-produced with Jean Waggoner for Epitome Records. It soon became clear from the vast amount of material which surfaced during our research that a literary anthology based on the city was more than justified.

Taking as my starting point Charles Whitby's useful work *The Bath Anthology* and C.P. Edwards' *Bath Bibliography* I then embarked on a part-time career as an amateur literary sleuth. This led me virtually to dis-embowell the Bath Reference Library's rich store of material. Of course any attempt to compile a comprehensive survey of literature relating to Bath would be impossible and certainly well beyond the aims of this book. I have therefore limited my choice to those pieces which I personally found exciting, unusual and with a fair degree of literary merit, avoiding where possible too much repetition in either style or content. I have also arranged the extracts chronologically according to the date of publication, keeping as close as I could to the original spelling and punctuation of the text contained in the earliest editions which I could lay my hands on.

To thank all those who have helped me over the years would require a great feat of memory on my part but special thanks must go to my friend Gill Atkins for all her support and encouragement without which this book would still be just an idea. My thanks must also go to Mary, Nicki, Peter, Julie and all the staff of the Bath Reference Library for all their patience and cheerfulness. Thanks also to Tom Clark who introduced me to Liz Boynton who introduced me to Penny Hargreaves who introduced me to Robin Campbell, my publisher. Thanks too must go to Linda Cresswell, Simon Hunt, Stephen Bird, Gill Knight and Anthony Addis for their advice and friendship.

Paul Cresswell
Bath

11

The Ruin

Wondrous is this masonry, shattered by the Fates. The City has been broken, and the fortifications raised by giants are crumbling. The roofs have fallen and the towers are in ruins. Fissures rent these roofless towers, and there is rime on the mortar. The battlements are mutilated and fallen to ruin, undermined by age. The master builders are perished and gone, held in the earth's embrace by the ruthless grip of the grave, whilst a hundred generations of mankind have passed away. Grey and red of hue with lichen this wall remained unmoved by storms throughout successive ages. The lofty arch has fallen into a shapeless mass within. ....This piece of antiquity skilfully wrought once shone with splendour....now broken asunder and encrusted with clay....With strength of purpose he marvellously clamped the walls by blows upon brazen rings. Glorious were the many palatial buildings of the city, its baths and high towered gables. Many were the banqueting halls full of mirth until all was shattered by obdurate Fate. The dead lay scattered on all sides. Pestilence came and all the warriors were carried off by death. Their fortresses became waste places, and the city decayed, and those who should have repaired them lay dead on the earth. Henceforth those dwellings crumbled away and large red tiles that shade the rafters of the roofs have fallen, cracked and broken among the ruins, where many a mailed warrior, merry and adorned in radiant gold, proud and flushed with wine, had looked on treasures of silver and precious stones, on untold wealth of gems, in this rich, spacious and magnificent city. There stood a stone enclosure where a wide, hot vapourous stream issued forth. A wall encompassed it within a bosom of splendor. There the baths contained the beneficent hot flood....The hot stream poured slowly over the grey stones from an unceasing whirlpool...until it reached the circular bath, whence it flowed...to the royal courthouse....

The Exeter Book
1072

ALEXANDER NECHAM

The Sacred Grove

The baths of Virgil scarce would I prefer
To those far-famed of Bath, for haply, there
The frail grow vigorous, the weakling strong,
And there the aged man once more grows young.
Those too find health who suffer ills untold,
That have their origin on the winter's cold,
Where Art discovers remedies too late
There Nature's laws man's toil anticipate.
Art's industry with Nature, both combined,
Oft much success and grand achievements find.
When Nature beckons, then doth follow Art
And both succeed, where one would fail in part.
So both to Nature and to Art 'twould seem
The baths are subject; for the waters' stream
Abounds with sulphur, called "the fire of earth"
And here it is the sulphur springs have birth.
Some say that in earth are pots, forsooth,
Of brass, which heat the waters. Is it truth?
It matters little whether false or true -
The sulphur's there, full well know I and you.
And yet amid the fumes sweet scents are there
Of cassia, bark, and cinnamon, and myrrh,
And with the plash of water all day long
Is heard the flute's clear melody of song,
A holy fame the place too seems to bear
For sancity's sweet odour fills the air.
Again I thirst, again I quick return,
And with the waters pure soon quench the burn.

In Praise of Divine Wisdom
1189

15

THOMAS CHAUNDLER
In Praise of Bath

Why should I speak of its situation? Nothing is more elegant and magnificent. Amongst its charms are shady groves, flowery meadows, pleasant streams, transparent fountains, and above all, the very nature of the place is formed for delight; for the very hills themselves by which the city is surrounded seem to smile and to diffuse a delight with which beholders cannot satisfy themselves, or be weary of surveying; so that the whole region round about may rightly be esteemed and named a sort of paradise, to which nothing in the whole world is equal in respect of beauty and delight. Allured by the fame of its beauty and for the sake of health, many persons resort to this city; and so much are they struck with its grandeur, its elegance, and its wealth, that they consider others as handmaids, but acknowledge this as mistress of the rest. The whole compass of the city is, in fine, encircled as by a coronet by a splendid wall; and, unless it be surveyed within, all its beauty cannot be beheld; for it has not less of beauty within its walls than without; nor are only one or two of its streets neat and elegant, but all its parts. What shall I say of the antiquity and nobility of its origin? Add to these the perennial flow of heated springs marvellously supplied for the benefit of man, over which, as Solinus says, Minerva presides, in whose temples perpetual fires never whiten into ashes; what can be more wonderful or more blessed than this provision by which all men, high and low, rich and poor, receive cure of all their maladies.

Libellus de Laudibus Civitatum
1452

Humilis thomas. C. alme Vniuersitatis Oxonie & ecclesie Ca
thedralis Wellñ Cancellari9; ad insigne dominū & beatissimū psulē
dominū thomā de bekintona Wellñ et bathoñ pontificem
sequñ cā psean opusculo & sua omnia.

Jo. Lelandus.

JOHN LELAND

Bath — A Pleasant Botom

Or ever I cam to the bridge of Bath that is over Avon I cam doun by a rokky hille fulle of fair springes of water: and on this rokky hille is sette a longe streate as a suburbe to the cyte of Bath: and (in) this streat is a chapelle of S. Mary Magdalen. Ther is a great gate with a stone arche at the entre of the bridge.

The bridge hath v. fair stone arches.

Bytwixt the bridge and the south gate of Bath I markid fair medows on eche hand, but especially on the lift hond, and they ly by south west on the toun.

The cite of Bath is sette booth yn a fruteful and pleasant botom, the which is environid on every side with greate hilles, out of the which cum many springes of pure water that be conveyid by dyverse ways to serve the cite. Insomuch that leade beyng made ther at hand many houses yn the toune have pipes of leade to convey water from place to place.

There be 4. gates yn the town by the names of est, west, north and south.

The toune waulle within the toune is of no great highth to theyes: but without it is *à fundamentis* of reasonable highth, and it stondith almost alle, lakking but a peace about Gascoyn's-tower.

...There be divers notable antiquitees engravid in stone that yet be sene yn the walles of Bathe betwixt the south gate and the weste gate: and agayn betwixt the west gate and the north gate.

The first was and antique hed of a man made al flat and having great lokkes of here as I have in a coine of C. Antius.

The secunde that I did se bytwene the south and the north gate was an image, as I looke it, of Hercules: for he held yn eche hand a serpent.

...The I saw ij. nakid imagis lying a long, the one imbracing the other.........

...Such antiquites as were in the waulles from the north gate to the est, and from the est gate to the south, hath been defacid by the building of the monastery, and making new waulles.

...There be 2. springes of whote wather in the west south west part of the towne. Wherof the bigger is caullid the Crosse Bath, bycause it hath a cross erectid in the midle of it. This bath is much frequentid of people deseasid with lepre, pokkes, scabbes, and great aches, and is temperate and pleasant, having a 11. or 12. arches of stone in the sides for men to stonde under yn tyme of reyne.

Many be holp by this bathe from scabbes and aches.

The other bathe is a 2. hunderith foote of, and is lesse in cumpace withyn the waulle then the other, having but 7. arches yn the waulle. This is caullid the Hote Bathe; for at cumming into it men think that it wold scald the flesch at the first, but after that the flesch ys warmid it is more tolerable and pleasaunt.

...The Kinges Bathe is very faire and large standing almost in the midle of the towne, and at the west end of the cathedrale chirch. ...The colour of the water of the baynes is as it were a depe blew se water, and rikth like a sething potte continually, having sumwhat a sulphureus and sumwhat onpleasant savor.

Leland's Itinerary
1540

JOHN JONES

Advice On Bathing

Every person going into the bathes, must fyrst clense ye bodies from superfluities. All persons affected or greeved by journey, shal not forthwith enter the bathes, but shal fyrst rest their bodies, by the space of a daye or two, yea or more.

...In the monethes of April, Maie, June, September, & October, when the ayer is temperate, be the best tymes.

About an howre after sunne rising, in the morninge, if the disseased require, drink the water out of the spring, the body afore purged, the digestion fulfilled, and the bath fyrst clensed, remaining cleane vi. houres before.

...The water being dronke, the partie must walke gentlie, a few paces, in a temperate ayer.

...And every person entring, shall fyrst emptie his bellie, and make water, if so be that he can not do that every day, yet every second or third daye.

Any person going into the Bathes, shal not sit in a place, somewhat distant from the spring, and so by lyttle & little draw towards the spring.

If ye parts under ye midrife be grieved, sit up to ye navel, but if ye parts above the navel be disseased, sit in unto the necke.

...See that altogither whyle ye be there, and lenger, yee avoyde copulation, that is, the use of women.

...When you come out, cover your selves with clothes, then go to bed, and sweate is convientient: but in the bath adstaine from slumbering.

When ye arise out of your bedde, or move in a place, free from distemperature of the ayer. especially the cold, and from the blasts of wynde.

The Booke of Bathes Ayde.

1572

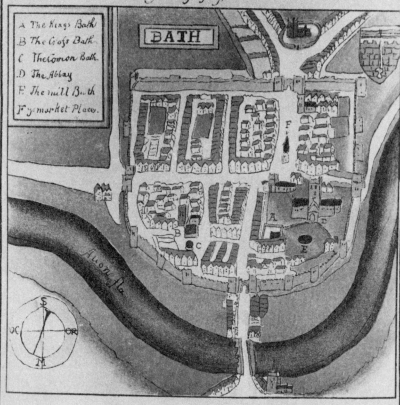

Somersethyre

| BATH |

A The Kings Bath
B The Goss Bath
C The comon Bath
D The Abbay
E The mill Bath
F ye market Place.

Avon fl.

S
OR
W · E
N

SLOANE MSS. No. 2596.

22

WILLIAM TURNER

A Treatise on the Baethe

Although there be a very excellent and holsome bath wythin the Realm of Englande,...there are manye...beynge diseased wyth sore diseases woulde gladlye come to the bath of Baethe: if they knewe that there were anye there, whereby they mighte be holpen, and yet knowe not whether there be anye in the Realme or no. ...The bath of England is in the West countre in Summerset-shire in a city called in Latin Bathonia, and Baethe in Englishe of the bathes, they are in it. This citie of Baethe is xv. miles from Welles, and xv. miles from the noble citye of Bristow. ...When as I was at these bathes wyth a certayn in the goute, I went in to them my selfe wyth my patiente, and broughte furth of the place nexte unto the spring, and out of thee bottom, slyme, mudde, bones and stones, whyche all together smelled...of brimstone. If that a man maye iudge the mater of the effect, maye gather that brimstone is the only mater in these bathes, or ellis the chefe that beareth ruel in them, for they drye up wounderfully, and heale the goute excellentlye. ...We maye gather that these ourse bathes are good for all those diseases, whyche all learned Phisicianes wryte that all other bathes, whose chefe ruler is brimstone...are good *for* the bathes of brimstone soften the synewes, and do heate. They are good therefore for palseyes, ...for the shaking and trimbling of anye membre...for the sciatica, and all ither ddiseases of the ioyntes...They scoure awaye frekels, and heale morfewes and scabbes. But they undo and overthrowe the stomack. ...When these bathes have ben of long tyme knowen, even above a thousand yeares, ether the unlearnednes or the enviousnes of the Pysiciones, which have ben in times past, is greatly to be rebuked, because ether for lak of learning knew not the vertues of these bathes, or els for enviusnes wold not send the sik folk, whom they could no otherwyse hele unto these bathes.

Treatise of the Bath
1562

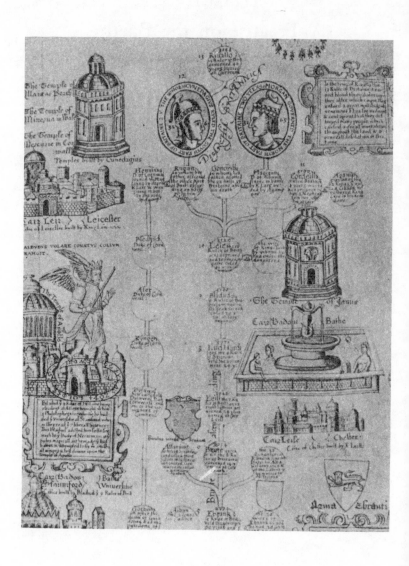

JOHN HIGGINS

Who Made The Baths At Bath

Some saye I made the batthes at Bathe:
And made therfore two tunnes of brasse:
And other twayne seuen slates that haue
In them, but these be made of glasse.

The water springes them rounde about,
Doth ryse for ay and boyleth still:
The tunnes within and eke without,
Do all the welles with vapoures fill.

So that the heate and clensing powre,
Of Sulpher and of salts and fyre:
Doth make the bathes eche pointed houre,
To helpe the sickly health desyre.

These bathes to soften sinewes haue
Great vertue and to scoure the skin:
From morphew white, and blacke to saue,
The bodies faint, are bathde therein.

For leprye, scabs, and sores are olde,
For scurfes, and botche, and humors fall:
The bathes haue vertues many folde,
If God giue grace to cure them all.

The ioyntes are swelde, and hardned milte:
And hardned liuer palseis paine,
The pore and itche, if worke thou wilt,
By helpe of God it heales againe.

Mirror for Magistrates
1574

EDMUND SPENCER

Beholde the Boyling Bathes

His sonne King *Leill* by fathers labour long,
    Enjoyd and heritage of lasting peace,
    And built *Cairleill,* and built *Cairleon* strong.
    Next *Huddibras* his realme did not encrease,
    But taught the land from wearie warres to cease.
    Whose footsteps *Bladud* following, in arts
    Exceld at *Athens* all the learned preace,
    From when he brought them to these saluage parts,
And with sweet science mollifide their stubborne harts.

Ensample of his wondrous faculty,
    Behold the boyling Bathes at *Cairbadon,*
    Which seeth with secret fire eternally,
    And in their entrails, full of quicke Brimston,
    Nourish the flames, which they are warm'd vpon,
    That to their people wealth they forth do well,
    And health to euery forreine nation:
    Yet he at last contending to excell
The reach of men, through flight into fond mischief fell.

The Faerie Queen
1579

WILLIAM STRODE

A Song on the Baths

What Angel stirrs this happy Well,
 Some Muse from thence come shew't me,
One of those naked Graces tell
 That Angles are for beauty:
The Lame themselves that enter here
 Come Angels out againe,
And Bodies turne to Soules all cleere,
 All made for joy, noe payne.

Heate never was so sweetley mett
 With moist as in this shower:
Old men are borne anew by swett
 Of its restoring pow'r:
When crippl'd joynts we suppl'd see,
 And second lives new come,
Who can deny this Font to be
 The Bodies Christendome?

One Bath so fiery is you'l thinke
 The Water is all Spirit,
Whose quick'ning streames are like the drink
 Whereby we Life inheritt:
The second Poole of middle straine
 Can wive Virginity,
Tempting the blood to such a vayne
 One sex is He and She.

The third where horses plunge may bring
 A Pegasus to reare us,
And call for pens from Bladud's wing
 For legging those that beare us.
Why should Physitians thither fly
 Where Waters med'cines be,
Physitians come to cure thereby,
 And are more cur'd than we.

    Poetical Works of William Strode
      1622

27

WILLIAM SHAKESPEARE

A Sovereign Cure
& a Healthful Remedy

Cupid laid by his brand and fell asleep,
A maid of Dian's this advantage found,
And his love-kindling fire did quickly steep
In a cold valley-fountain of that ground,
Which borrow'd from this holy fire of love
A dateless lively heat, still to endure,
And grew a seething bath, which yet men prove
Against strange maladies a sovereign cure.
But at my mistress' eye Love's brand new-fir'd,
The boy for trial needs would touch my breast;
I, sick withal, the help of bath desir'd,
And thither hied, a sad distemper'ed guest,
    But found no cure; the bath for my help lies
    Where Cupid got new fire — my mistress' eyes.

The little love-god lying once asleep
Laid by his side his heart inflaming brand,
Whilst many nymphs that vow'd chaste life to keep
Came tripping by; but in her maiden hand
The fairest votary took up that fire,
Which many legions of true hearts had warm'd;
And so the general of hot desire
Was sleeping by a virgin hand disarm'd.
This brand she quenched in a cool well by,
Which from Love's fire took heat perpetual,
Growing a bath, and healthful remedy
For men diseas'd; but I, my mistress' thrall,
    Came there for cure, and this by that I prove:
    Love's fire heats water, water cools not love.

Sonnets
1609

28

ANONYMOUS
The Cock-pit City

"Bath City. To this Citty wee came late and wet, and entred stumbling into a third Cock-pit City, over a fayre archt Bridge crossing Avon: She may well be turn with her Sister Wells, both for her Scytuation & her Governmt; and heere wee billetted or selves at the 3 Tuns, close to the King's Bath. — And now prepared wee, wth the skillfull directions of our Ancient, to take apreparative to fit or jumbled weary corps to enter & take refreshmt in those admired, unapparalell'd, medicinable sulphurous, hot bathes: There wee met all kind of Persons, of all shapes & fformes, of all degrees, of all countryes, & of all Diseases of both Sexes; for to see young and old, rich and poore; blind & lame, diseas'd & sound; english & ffrench, men & women; boys and & girles, one wth another peepe up in their caps, & appeare so fearefully, in their uncouth postures, would a little astonish & put one in mind of the Resurrection. ffor or parts we found the pleasure of it, and the better it was for us, through the great care of our diligent attendant, more indeed then any benefit wee found, for ayling nothing, it produc'd neither good nor harme to us, yet sure to such as stand in need of this place, & the sulphurous waters, it brings exceeding great ease to such, and much content too. "To leave them, let us speake a little of the towne: it is govern'd by a Scarlet Major, & his 11 Brethren, 2 Maces; & is seated in a deepe bottome, & neere 3 quarters thereof invironed wth that sweet gliding Streame, that comes from Malmesbury, & funs to Bristow, wall'd most about (exccept that part that the river hems in) wth as many gates to enter her, as her inhabitants have churches for them to enter, & just soe many rare Bathes springing up in her."

"Close to this Church are 2 curious Bowling Grounds, one of them is curiously and neatly kept, where onely Lords, Knights, Gallants, & Gentlemen, of the best ranke and qualitie doe dayly meet in seasonable times to recreate themselves; both for pleasure and health: And likewise neere unto her there is situated a fayre Building retayning still the venerable name of an Abbey."

"By this it was high time to depart from this deare place and indeed here we parted, from the Captaine and Anceint tooke their way over the bridge againe to that famous City of Salisbury, and on went the Lieutenant alone toward the ancient old unconquer'd maiden towne of Malmesbury, out at the North Gate, whereon stands King Bladud's Statue, who first founded these precious Bathes, 900 yeeres before or Saviour' Incarnation, through that Street where that fayre ffree Stone Crosse of 20 Pillars standeth."

A Short Survey of Twenty-Six Counties
1634

MICHAEL DRAYTON

Minerva's Sacred Spring

Then Bradon gently brings forth Avon from her source:
Which Southward making soone in her most quiet course,
Receives the gentle Calne; when on her rising side,
First Blackmoore crownes her banke, as Peusham with her
pride
Sets out her murmuring sholes, till (turning to the West)
Her, Somerset receives, with all the bounties blest
That Nature can produce in that Bathonian Spring,
Which from the Sulphury Mines her med'cinall force doth
bring;
As Physick hath found out by colour, taste and smell,
What quickliest it could cure: which men of knowledge drew
From that first minerall cause: but some that little knew
(Yet felt the great effects continually it wrought)
Ascrib'd it to that skill, which Bladud hither brought,
As by that learned King the Bathes should be begunne;
Not from the quickned Mine, by the begetting Sunne
Giving that natural power, which by the vig'rous sweate,

Doth lend the lively Springs their perdurable heate
In passing through the veines, where matter doth not need;
Which in that minerous earth insep'rably doth breed:
So nature hath pervai'd, that during all her raigne
The Bathes their native power for ever shall retaine:
Where Time that Citie built, which to her greater fame,
Preserving of that Spring, participates her name;
The Tutilage whereof (as those past worlds did please)
Some to Minerva gave, and some to Hercules:
Proud Phoebus loved Spring, in whose Diurnall course,
When on this point of earth he bends his greatest force,
By his so strong approach, provokes her to desire;
Stung with the kindly rage of loves impatient fire:
Which boiling in her wombe, projects (as to a birth)
Such matters as she takes from the grosse humorous earth;
Till purg'd of dregs and slime, and her complexion cleere,
She smileth on the light, and lookes with mirthful cheere.
  Then came the lustie Froome, the first of floods that met
Faire Avon, entring in to fruitful Somerset,
With her attending Brooks; and her to Bathe doth bring,
Much honoured by that place, Minerva's sacred Spring.

Poly-Olbion Song III
1613

HENRY JACOB

Bathonia

Bright *Apollo*, who dost shine
The *Numen* of sweet Medicine;
From whose golden lockes destill
Balmy drops to cure each ill:
Still defend thou from all scath
The boyling springs of famous *Bath*.
Let the waining Moones faint beames
Command the course of chiller streams,
The constant and inconstant Guide
Of the reciprocating Tide.
These be Thine; exempted free
From th'other wett fraternitie;
By our Auncients long agon
Stil'd the *Waters of the Sun*
IO PAEAN! A good Spirit
Doth these sovrainge waves inherit:
Founts, that have an easing trick
Not for the thirsty, but the sick
Emp'rick's and booke-prompted *Soiphi's*
Adore here Aesculapian Trophies;
The propping *crutch*, the swadling tie,
And what recovered strengths lays by.
Oyes, crayzie! Com and follow
To this health-market of *Apollo*.
Who in-Griefs rack, or out-Sores pester,
Goe or creep to *Akemanchester*.

Jacob's Philogiae
1653

THOMAS WEAVER

A Letany Upon A Journey To Bath

From going to Bath with little money in my purse;
From staying there after all's spent, which is worse
And from a drawers visit when I'm ready to horse,
                    Good Mercury defend me.

From an old German Quack yclipp'd Doctor Bavie,
Whose skill is not half so much as his knavery,
And ten to one will rather kill 'ee than save 'ee,
                    Good Mecury defend me.

From his Purges and Vomits, his Powders and Jellie,
With more for's own good then yours he does sell 'ee,
And from medling with the Tapsters wife with a great belly,
                    Good Mercury defend me.

From Ladies that take Phisick before they be sick;
That they may with better mettal answer the prick,
Who copulate thrice a night, yet call't a lewd trick,
                    Good Mercury defend me.

From such as in Bath use to sing a Hymn,
From such a Barber that on Sunday mornings refuses to trim,
From living a traitor, and dying like Pym,
                    Good Mercury defend me.

From a Colonel that vapours as if he were Mars,
Yet will take a blow on the face, and a kick on the arse,
And so suffers more in Peace than he did in the Wars.,
                    Good Mercury defend me.

                    Songs and Poems of Love and Drollery.
                    1654

35

SAM·PEPYS·CAR·ET·IAC·ANGL·REGIB·A·SECRETIS·ADMIRALIÆ·

SAMUEL PEPYS

A Peep At The Bath

12th June 1668

Having dined very well — we came home before night to the
Bath. Where I presently stepped out with my landlord and saw
the baths with people in them. They are not so large as I expected but yet pleasent and the town most of stone and clean
though the streets generally narrow. I home and being weary
went home to bed without supper the rest supping.

13th June

Up at 4 a'clock being by appointment called up to the (Cross)
Bath where we were carried after one another myself and wife
and Betty Turner *Willet* and *WH*. And by and by though we
designed to have done before company came much company
came very fine ladies and the manner pretty enough only
methinks it cannot be clean to go so many bodies together in
to the same water. Good conversation among them that are ac-
quainted here and stay together. Strange to see how hot the
water is and in some places though this is the most temperate
bath the springs so hot as the feet not to endure. But strange
to see what women and men herein that live all the season in
these waters that cannot but be parboiled and look like
creatures of the Bath. Carried back wrap in a sheet and in a
chair home and there one after another thus carried (I staying
above two hours in the water) home to bed seating for an hour
and by and by comes music to play to me extraordinary good
as ever I heard at London almost anywhere.

14th June

Up and walked and down the town and saw a pretty good
market place and many good street and very fair stone houses
and so to (the *great church*) and there saw *Bp* Montagu's tomb
and when placed did there see many brave people come and
among other two men brought in litters and set down in the
chancel to hear. But I did not know one face. Here a good

Organ but a vain pragmatic fellow preached a ridiculous sermon affected that made me angry and some *gent* that sat next me and sang well. So home walking round the walls of the city which are good and the *battlements* all whole.

15th June

Up and with Mr. *Butts* to look into the Baths and find the King and Queen's full of a mixed sort of good and bad and the Cross only almost for the gentry. So home and did the like with my wife and did pay my guides. Before I took coach, I went to make a boy dive in the King's Bath — 1 shilling.

Samuel Pepy's Diary
1668

NED WARD

A Step to the Bath

Having Din'd, we proceeded on our Journey, but with a great deal
of difficulty; for the Road was so Rocky, Unlevel, and Narrow in
some Places, that I am persuaded the *Alps* are to be passed with
less danger... At last when our Patience was almost worn out... our
Charioteer inform'd us we were at our Journeys-end, ...and *Bath*
was as welcome to us as a good Dinner to a *Convent-Garden Tooth-
picker*.... At the *Three-Tuns*, ...we enliven'd our Souls with a Glass
of good *Burdeaux* and Sparkling *Sherry; and from thence we went to
see the Diversions of the Baths.*

...The first we went to, is call'd the *Kings*, and it joyns the *Queens*,
both running in one; and the most Famous for Cures. In this *Bath*
was at least Fifty of both Sexes, with a Score or two of Guides, who
by their *Scorbutick Carcases* and *Lacker'd Hides*, you would think
they had lain Pickling a *Century* of *Years in the Stygian-Lake*... In
one Corner was and Old Fornicator hanging by the Rings, loaded
with a *Rotten Humidity:* Hard by him was a Buxom Dame, cleaning
her *Nunquam Satis* from *Mercurial Dregs... Another, half cover'd with
Searcloth,* had more Sores than *Lazarus,* doing Pennance for the Sins
of her Youth; at her Elbow as a Young hero, supported by a couple
of Guides, Rack'd with *Aches* and *Intollerable* Pains...

From thence we went to the *Cross-Bath,* where most of the Quality resorts, more Fam'd for *Pleasure* than *Cures....* Here is perform'd
all the *Wanton Dalliancies* imaginable: *Celebrated Beauties, Panting
Breasts,* and *Curious Shapes* almost expos'd to Publick View;
Languishing Eyes, Darting Killing Glances, Tempting Amourous Postures,
attended by soft *Musick,* enough to provoke a *Vestal* to *Forbidden
Pleasure....* The vigorous Sparks, presenting them with several An-
tick Postures, as Sailing on their Backs, then Embracing the Elements,
sink in a Rapture and by Accidental Design, thrust a stretch'd Arm;
but where the Water conceal'd, so ought my Pen.

A Step to the Bath
1700

40

CELIA FIENNES

The Wayes To The Bath

The wayes to the Bath are all difficult, the town lyes Low in a bottom and its steep ascents all wayes out of the town. The houses are indifferent, the streetes of a good size well pitched. There are severall good houses built for Lodgings that are new and adorned, and good furniture, the baths in my opinion makes the town unpleasant, the aire so low, encompassed with high hills and woods. There is 5 baths the hot bath the most hot springs — its but small and built all round, which makes it ye hotter — out if it runns the water into a bath called the Le pours.

The third bath is called the Cross bath which is some thing bigger then the former and not so hot.

...The Kings bath is very large, ...in it is the hot pumpe that persons are pumpt at for Lameness or on their heads for palsyes. I saw one pumpt, they put on a broad brim'd hatt with the Crown cut out so as ye brims Cast off ye water from ye face. So... The Ladyes goes into the bath with Garments made of a fine yellow canvas, which is stiff and made large with great sleeves like a parsons gown... The Gentlemen have drawers and waistcoates of the same sort of canvas.

...Ye queens bath is a degree hotter than ye Cross bath and ye Kings bath much hotter, these have all galleryes round and the pump is in one of these gallery's at ye Kings bath which ye Company drinks of, it is very hot and tastes like the water that boyles Eggs, has such a smell, but ye nearer the pumpe you drink it, ye hotter and less offencive and more spiriteous.

...Ye places for divertion about ye bath is either ye walkes in that they call ye Kings Mead which is a pleasant green meaddow, where are walkes round and Cross it, no place for Coaches,...for ye wayes are not proper for Coaches.

Ye town and all its accomodations is adapted to ye batheing and drinking of the waters and to nothing else...there are Chaires as in London to Carry ye better sort of people in visits, or if sick or infirme and is only in the town, for it is so Encompassed with high hills few care to take the aire on them.

The Diary of Celia Fiennes
1687

41

RICHARD STEELE

An Intelligence From The Bath

Having had several strange pieces of intelligence from the Bath; as, that more consitutions were weakened there than repaired; that the physicians were not more busy in destroying old bodies, than the young fellows were in producing new ones; with several other... strokes of rallery: I resolved to look upon the company there, as I returned lately out of the country. It was a great jest to see such a grave ancient person, as I am in an embroidered cap and brocade nightgown. But, besides the necessity of complying with the custom, by these means I passed undiscovered, and had a pleasure, I much covet, of being alone in a crowd. It was no little satisfaction to me, to view the mixt mass of all ages and dignities upon a level, partaking of the same benefits of nature, and mingling in the same diversions. I sometimes entertained myself, by observing what a large quantity of ground was hid under spreading petticoats; and what little patches of earth were covered by creatures with wigs and hats, in comparison to those spaces that were distinguished by flounces, fringes and fallbullows. From the earth, my fancy was diverted to the water, where...the mixture of men and women hath given occasion to some persons of light imaginations, to compare the Bath to...the stream wherein Diana washed herself, when she bestowed horns on Acteon. But by one of a serious turn, these healthful springs may rather by likened to the Stygian waters, which made the body invulnerable; or to the river of Lethe, one draught of which washed away all pain and anguish in a moment.

The Guardian

1713

The Bath Medley

The Springs a coming and Natures a blooming each Amorous Lover does Vigour recover

Birds are Singing & Flowers are Springing heres Toys to be Raffled for who makes one

(2)
Best past comparisons
At Mr Harrisons
Dice are rattling
Beaus are Pratling
Ladies walking
And wittily talking
Madam the Medleys
Iust begun

(3)
Heres half a Guinea
To hear Nicolini
Come give me a Ticket
Main's Seven nine Nicks it
I'm going to Lindseys
Spadilla wins Ye
I'm beat by Ierico
quite undone

(4)
Bells are Iangling
Chair Men wrangling
Cudgelling Thumping
Bathing and Pumping
The way of the Morning
Is Dreſing adorning
And then to the Green
where the Laſses Run

(5)
Pray Madam bespeak
Or the Play Houſe will break
We have had a bad Season
And hope for that Reason
You wont see Three
In the whole Company
That can Act You to Sleep
Tho You had the Gout

(6)
Well Strutt You Cato
Or Speeches of Plato
Farce Comedy Paſtorall
Wacan maſter all
Like St Martin
We chatter each Part in
And never Stop till the Speech
ist out

(7)
Pray lets wheele Ye
Damn the Medley
Woud Sombody poiſon him
Well raiſe lies on him
Pit Box Gallery
Its better then Raillery
Were pretty Gentlem
Hes a Lout

(8)
Thus they teize Ye
And never can pleaſe Ye
With Actions Improper
So Huff it in Copper
Theres Sons of the Garret
Theſe Chatter like Parrot
And Scatter their Calumny
all about

(9)
Heres Punch Shews at Five
And heres Craw Fiſh alive
Some Eaſtward ſome Northw
Stalk backward and forward
While others so Stingy
Penny Pott it with Bingy
And Hey for the Race
Clerken Down

(10)
On Lanſſoan Airing
The Footmen Swearing
Ingeniously waiting
To see Badger Baiting
Damning Dangling
Prancing Angling
Each has his M...
unto the Crown

(11)
Some are Bowling
Or Eunuchs howling
Some Subſcribing
Or Briſtol Milk bibing
We've had many a Fit
At my Sons Benifit
Pleaſe to Put in for ..
Indian Gown

(12)
Who'll play at Billiards
Fair as Stillyards
Heres a couple of Calves Sr
Come Ill go Your halues Sr
There they Hole them
And put in and pole them
And theſe are the Ways
Of Bathing Town

(13)
All Sorts of Conditions
Cits Lawyers Phyſitians
Both good ones and bad ones
The Sober and Mad ones
Some to meet their old Friend
And for Various Ends
Are Galloping hither
twice a Year

(14)
Heres King Edgar and Kaole
And Poppet Show Powel
Once Perſons so great
Tho now out of Date
Mind the Changes of things
From Poppets to Kings
And what may be one Day
the Medleys Fate

(15)
Sr Fr to the Ball
And there You may Call
Advance with Authority
Parionszto Dorothy
Richmond Wells
Or the Iriſh Bells
And Foot it about
With the Ladies all

(16)
Then to the three Tuns
The Queens head or Rummer
Adieu Ye Fair ones
Till Tunbridge at Summer
Pray Maiters away
For the Coach cannot Stay
Your welcome Gentlemen
to the Bear

For the FLUTE

ANONYMOUS

The Pleasures Of The Bath

The *Spring's* a coming, And *Nature's* a blooming;
Each amourous Lover does Vigour recover:
The Birds are singing, And Flowers are springing;
Here's Toys to be raffl'd for, who makes one?

Best, past *Comparisons*, At Mr *Harrison's*;
Dice are rattling, Beaus are prattling,
Ladies walking, And wittily talking;
Madam the *Medly's* just begun.

Bells are jangling, Chairmen rangling,
Cudgelling, Thumping, Bathing and Pumping;
The way of the Morning Is Dressing, Adorning;
And then to the Green where the Lasses run.

Pray Madam bespeak, Or the Playhouse must break,
We've had a bad Season, and hope for that Reason.
You wont see three, For a whole Company
that will act you to sleep, tho' you had the Gout.

All sorts of Conditions, City-Lawyers, Physicians,
Both good ones and bad ones, the sober and mad ones;
Some to meet their old Friends, And for various Ends,
Are galloping hither twice a Year.

Sir, up to the Ball, And there you may call,
A Dance with Authority, Parson upon Dorithy,
Richmond Wells, Or Irish Bells,
And foot it about with the Ladies.

Then to the Three-Tuns, Queen's Head or the Rummer;
Adieu, ye fair ones 'Till Tunbridge at Summer;
Come hasten away, For the Coach cannot stay;
You're welcome Gentlemen at the bear.

A Broadside
1716

45

THOMAS DURFEY

On A Lady's Going Into The Bath

When *Sylvia* in her Bathing, her Charms does expose,
The pretty Banquet dancing under her Nose;
My heart is just ready to part from my Soul,
And leap from the Ga....'ry into the Bowl:
      Each day I provide too,
      A bribe for her Guide too,
      And gave her a Crown,
To bring me the Water where she sat down;
Let crazy Physitians think Pumping a Cure,
That Virtue is doubtful, but *Sylvia's* is sure.

The Fidlers I hire to play something Sublime,
And all the while throbbing my Heart beats the Time;
She enters, they Flourish, and cease when she goes,
That who it is address'd to, straight ev'ry one knows;
      Wou'd I were a Vermin,
      Call'd one of her Chairmen,
      Or serv'd as a Guide
Tho' show'd as they do a damn'd tawny Hide,
Or else like a Pebble at bottom cou'd lye,
To Ogle her Beauties, how happy were I.

Pills to Purge Melancholy
1719

ANONYMOUS

On The Promiscuous Mixture Of Company, And The Various Humours Of Persons In The Hot Baths, At Bath In Somersetshire.

In reeking *Bath* promiscuous Crowds we view,
Alike both sexes here their Ease persue.
Here some repair to captivate, in Chains
Youths hold, and some are pump'd for Achs & Pains;
Here brawny Back, there Skeleton appears,
A sporting Lass, a Lady gay in Years;
In finest Dress each Female's Head attir'd,
All equal Care still take to be admir'd;
Plump heaving Breasts are in their beauty seen,
More white than Snow, beneath the Waters clean;
Each face with Blush the Sulph'rous Heat inspires:
No ruddy Paint the Female here requires.
Fine Handkerchief in swimming Toy's display'd,
In it a Dram and Essence-Vial laid.
The Minerals drank, here some their vertues praise;
In Depths conceal'd the healing Waters raise:
The Noble Spring increases in its Worth,
By Briny Floods from Nature gushing forth.
The Bath oft traversd, nor possess'd with Cares,
To well-rang'd Nich a Dutchess here repairs:
The Canvas Smock now, at the Bottom wide,
Is high display'd by lusty Female Guide;
Each Part she rubs, obsequious to Command,
To Labour us'd, like Brush is felt her Hand.
If by some Youth this office was posses'd,
What Parts then wou'd be rubb'd, are easy to be guess'd.

A Lovers Miscellany
1719

DANIEL DEFOE

Diversions Of Bath

My description of this City would be very short, and indeed it would have been a very small City, (if at all a city) were it not for the *Hot Baths* here, which give both Name and Fame to the Place.

The Antiquity of this Place, and of the *Baths* here, is doubtless very great, tho' I cannot come in to the Inscription under the figure, said to be of a Brittish King, placed in that call'd the King's *Bath*, which says that this King *Bladud*, ...found out the use of these *Baths*, 300 Years before our Saviour's Time.

...There remains little to add, but what relates to the Modern Customs, the Gallantry and Diversions of that Place, in which I shall be very short; the best Part being but a Barren Subject, and the worst Part meriting rather a Satyr than a Description.

It has been observ'd before, that in former Times this was a Resort hither for Cripples, and the Place was truly Urbs *Aegrotorum Hominum;* And we see the Crutches hang up at the several Baths, as the Thank-Offerings of those who have come hither Lame and gone away Cured. But now we may say it is the Resort of the Sound, rather than the Sick; the Bathing is made more a Sport and Diversion, than a Physical Prescription for Health; and the Town is taken up in Raffling, Gameing, Visiting, and in a Word, all sorts of Gallantry and Levity.

The whole time indeed is a Round of the utmost Diversion. In the Morning you (supposing you to be a young Lady) are fetch'd in a close Chair, dress'd in you Bathing Cloths, that is, stript to the Smock, to the *Cross-Bath.* There the Musick plays you into the the Bath and the Women that tend you, present you with a little floating Wooden Dish, like a Bason; in which the Lady puts a Handkerchief, and a Nosegay, of late the Snuff-Box is added, and some Patches; tho' the Bath occasioning a little Perspiration, the Patches do not stick so kindly as they should.

Here the Ladies and Gentlemen pretend to keep some distance, and each to their proper Side, but frequently mingle here too, as in the King and Queens Bath, tho' not so often; and the Place being but narrow, they converse freely, and talk, rally, make Vows, and sometimes Love; and having thus amus'd themselves an Hour, or Two, they call their Chairs and return to their Lodgings.

The rest of the Diversion here, is the Walks in the great Church, and at the Raffling shops, which are kept (like the cloister at *Bartholomew* Fiar,) in the Churchyard and, ground adjoyning . In the Afternoon there is generally a Play, tho' the Decorations are mean and the Performances accordingly; but it answers, for the Company here (not the Actors) make the Play, to say no more. In the Evening there is a Ball, and Dancing at least twice a week, which is commonly in the great Town Hall over the Market-House; where there never fails in the Season to be a great deal of a very good Company.

Tour Thro' The Whole British Isles.
1724

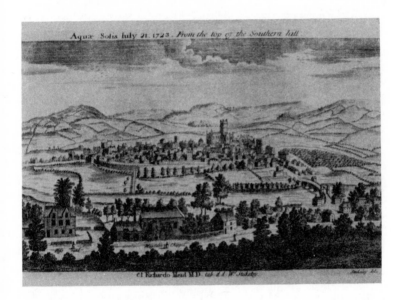

49

WILLIAM CONGREVE

Orders Of His Excellency R.....d N... Esq, Governor General Of The Diversions At Bath

Some come here for pleasure and others for health.
Some come here to squander, and some to get wealth.
To those all our subjects here merrily meeting, —
We Governor Nash — do send out our Greeting

Whereas it to us has been fully made known
Some queer folks presume to have wills of their own
And think when they come to such places as these —
They've unlimited licence to do as they please.

When'ere frequent disorders do daily arise
To prevent such abuses what 'ere in us lyes
We publish these rules considered at leisure
And expect due observance, for such is our pleasure.

When you first come to Bath, in whatever condition,
Whether sick of in health, you must have a Physitian,
As they'll equally take inordinate fees
You're at your own liberty, choose whom you please.

The Doctor will find there is absolute need
That friend Jerry Pierce must be sent for to bleed.
Next, some drops or some pills prepared with due care
To prevent all infection from water or air
Then drink at the pump or bathe without feare.

When you first Sally out there are different calls
At Hayes's or Lovelace's, money for Balls
As nothing in this world is done without Bribe,
Leake, Sinnott or Morgan Expect you'll Subscribe.

When this part is over then live at your Ease,
Game, drink or fornicate just as your please.
When your money is spent march off without trouble,
Secure, who comes next will be just the same Bubble.

Miscellaneous Papers 1728

ANONYMOUS

The Diseases Of Bath

If to the Pump-room in the morn we go
To drink the waters and remove some woe;
Idle the project We too late explore;
And find: to move one Plague, we've dar'd a score.
What tumult, hurry, noise and nonsense blend,
T'annoy the senses, and the Soul t'ofend!
What sickly, crude, offensive Vapours there
The nostils snuff up with the tainted air!
Whole groups of Foppish slovens foully fine
In dirty shirts, and tinsul stink and shine;
Midst crowds of Dames, who in their nightly trim,
Just reeking from their beds, still stew and steam:
An ill-bred, restless, wild and crackling host,
Noisy as Goslings spreading from their roost.

Shock'd at the Light and Sound I onward rush
To whence th' up-driven Streams, hot smoaking gush:
Forc'd to wade thro' a Mob of unwash'd Beaus
At th' ill expence of elbows and of cloaths.
By patient squeezing to the Pump I get;
There roughly thrust next to some Clown I wait;
Who, when he'as rudely swilled his Potion up,
Leaves me the slobber'd favour of his Cup.
Urg'd by despair I plunge into the Bath,
But! — here still heavier Plagues insense my wrath.
Nameless Diseases join'd pollute the Stream,
Here long e'er Lucifer leads the Dawn,
Each greasy Cook has seeth'd away his Brawn;
And Sweepers from thair Chimnies, smear'd with Soot,
Hither have brought, and left behind, their smut.
Jilts, Porters, Grooms, and Guides, and Chairmen bring
Their sev'ral Ordure to corrupt the Spring.
Add to these nusances the 'wild'ring Noise
Of splashing Swimmers, and of dabbling Boys;
Whose bold, loose, rustick gestures move my Rage,
Which Celia's pressence scarcely can asswage.

Here Lepra too, and Scabies more unclean
Divest their Scurf t'invest a purer Skin;
Whose pealing Scales upon the surface swim,
Till what th'unwholesome shed the Wholesome skim.
Nor this the greatest Grievence in the Flood:
The worst I scarcely wish were understood:
All (from the Porter to the courtly Nymph)
Pay liquid tributes to the swelling Lymph.
What benefit such Mixtures can impart:
To know — or ev'n to guess — is past my Art.

1737

JOHN MACKY

The Company At Bath

The Bath lies very low; is but a small city, but very compact; and one can hardly imagine it could accommodate near the Company that frequents it, at three parts of the year. I have been told of 8,000 families there at a time, some for the benefit of drinking its hot waters, others for bathing, and others for diversion and pleasure; of which I must say, it affords more than any publick place of that kind in Europe.

I told you in my former letters that Epsom and Tunbridge does not allow visiting; the companies there meet only on the walks; but here vists are received and returned, Assemblies and Balls are given, and parties at Play in most houses every night, to which Mr. Nash hath for many years contributed very much. This Gentleman is by custom a sort of Master of Ceromonies of the Place; he is not of any birth, nor Estate, but by a good address and Assurance ingratiates himself into the good graces of the Ladies, and the best company in the place, and is Director of all their parties of Pleasure. He wears good cloaths, is always affluent of Money, plays very much; and whatever he may get in private, yet in publick he always seems to lose. The Town have been for many years so sensible of the service he does them, that they ring bells generally at his arrival in Town, and, 'tis thought, pay him a yearly contribution for his support.

I have often wondered that the Physicians of these places prescribe Gaming to their patients, in order to keep their minds free from business and thought, that their Waters on an undisturbed mind may have the greater Effect; when indeed one cross throw at Play must sowre a Man's blood more than ten Glasses of Water will sweeten, especially for such great sums as they throw for every day at Bath.

A Journey through England
1714

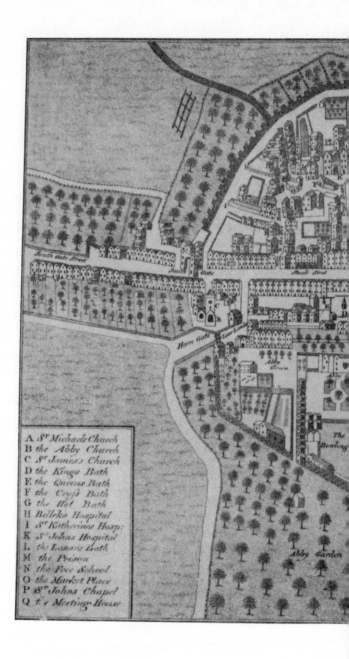

A S.ᵗ Michaels Church
B the Abby Church
C S.ᵗ James's Church
D the Kings Bath
E the Queens Bath
F the Crofs Bath
G the Hot Bath
H Belleks Hospital
I S.ᵗ Katherines Hosp:
K S.ᵗ Johns Hospital
L the Lazars Bath
M the Prison
N the Free School
O the Market Place
P S.ᵗ Johns Chapel
Q the Meeting House

HENRY FIELDING

An Extempore In The Pump Room
To Miss H.... And At Bath

SOON shall these bounteous springs thy wish bestow
Soon in each feature sprightly health shall glow:
Thy eyes regain their fire, thy limbs their grace
And roses join the lilies in thy face.
But say, sweet maid, what waters can remove
The pangs of cold despair, of hopeless love?
The deadly star which lights th' autumnal skies
Shines not so bright, so fatal as those eyes.
The pains which from their influence we endure.
Not *Brewster* glory of his art, can cure.

Micellaneous Poems
1742

ANONYMOUS

An Easy Cure

or a Prescription for an Invalid when at BATH

If, Brother Hyp, you want a Cure,
At BATH a Lodging warm secure;
There drink the wholsome Stream by Rule,
When Nature's Stream runs low and cool.

Arise betime, to Pump repair,
First take the Water, then the Air;
Then stroll to Coffee-House, - peruse,
With Air of Negligence, the News;

Not caring whether Party rules;
Provided no rebellious Tools
Disturb the Nations public Peace,
To interrupt your private Ease.

Frequent the Church, in decent Dress,
There offer up religious Vows;
Yourself to none but GOD address;
Avoiding foppish Forms and Bows.

When you've your due Devotions paid,
Walk on the North or South Parade;
If Weather's clear, in Sun and Air,
The best of Whets for Foodprepair.

Then sparing take, of lightest kind,
To keep the Vessels free from Wind;
In Wine and Sauces don't exceed;
Luxurious Tastes Distempers breed.

Nature refresht, let Nature rest;
With inward Peace your Mind digest,
Digestion's Work is easiest wrought,
By cheerful Chat and little Thought:

Or, to disperse black Fumes away,
At Whisk or Ombre cheerful play;
Be unconcern'd at Loss or Gain;
A Spirit ruffled, raises Pain.

The Mind unbent, your Thought prepare,
Tom bear a Part in Ev'ning Pray'r:
The Duty done, a Draught repeat,
Concoction help with liquid Heat.

Thence lounge at Coffee-House, in Chat,
On various Themes of God knows what;
'Till two or more, of friendly Kind,
Of Nature good, of cheerful Mind,
In Sense and Mirth agree to pass
The Time 'till Nine, in circling Glass;
Thence Home to Sleep; and rise next Light,
With Spirits lively, gay and bright.

Thus Invalids, from Day to Day,
Must keep like Clocks in constant Way;
Must modest be in Meat and Drink,
And rarely (very rarely) think.

Must excercise with gentle Force,
On Foot, or Coach, or pacing Horse;
Must rise and set at early Hours,
And ne'er exert beyond their Powers.

This Course observ'd will Thousands save
from Pain, from Anguish, and the Grave.-
Pills Nature vex, and weaken too;
These Rules of Health the Man renew.

The New Bath Guide
1761

OLIVER GOLDSMITH
A Faint Picture Of Bath

The city of Bath, by such assiduity, soon became the theatre of summer amusements for all people of fashion; and the manner of spen-
ding the day there must amuse any but such as disease or spleen
has made uneasy to themselves. The following is a faint picture of
the pleasures that scene affords. Upon a stranger's arrival at Bath,
he is welcomed by a peal of the abbey bells, and in the next place
by the voice and music of the city waits....These customs, though
disagreeable, are however generally liked, or they would not continue. The greatest incommodity attending them is the disturbance
the bells must give the sick. But the pleasure of knowing the name
of every family that comes to town recompenses the inconvenience.
Invalids are fond of news, and upon the first sound of the bells
everybody sends out to inquire for whom they ring.

After the family is thus welcomed to Bath, it is the custom for
the master of it to go to the public places, and subscribe two guineas
at the assembly-houses towards the balls and music in the pump-
house, for which he is entitled to three tickets every ball night.

...Things being thus adjusted, the amusements of the day are
generally begun by bathing, which is no unpleasing method of passing
away an hour or so....The hours for bathing are commonly between
six and nine in the morning, and the baths are every morning supplied with fresh water.

...The amusement of bathing is immediately succeeded by a
general assembly of people at the pump-house, some for pleasure,
and some to drink the hot waters. Three glasses, at three different
times, is the usual portion for every drinker; and the intervals between every glass are enlivened by the harmony of a small band of
music, as well as by the conversation of the gay, the witty, or the
forward.

From the Pump-house the ladies, from time to time, withdraw
to a female coffee-house, and from thence return to their lodgings
to breakfast. The gentlemen withdraw to their coffee-houses to read
the papers, or converse on the news of the day with a freedom and
ease not to be found in the metropolis....

...Thus we have the tedious morning fairly over. When noon
approaches, and church (if any please to go there) is done, some
of the company appear upon the parade, and other public walks,

where they continue to chat and amuse each other, till they have formed parties for the play, cards, or dancing for the evening. Some walk in the meadows around the town, winding along the side of the river Avon and the neighbouring canal; while others are seen scaling some of those romantic precipices that overhang the city....

...After dinner is over, and evening prayers ended, the company meet a second time at the pump-house. From this they retire to the walks, and from thence go to drink tea at the assembly-houses,

and the rest of the evenings are concluded either with balls, plays or visits. ...Thus Bath yields a continued rotation of diversions, and people of all ways of thinking, even from the libertine to the methodist, have it in their power to complete the day with employments suited to their inclinations.

The Life Of Richard Nash Of Bath, Esq.,
1762

TOBIAS SMOLLETT
The Terrors Of Bathing

I have done with the waters; therefore your advice comes a day too late....Two days ago, I went into the King's Bath, by the advice of our friend Ch...., in order to clear the strainer of the skin, for the benefit of a free perspiration; and the first object that saluted my eye, was a child full of scrophulous ulcers, carried on the arms of one of the guides, under the very noses of the bathers. I was so shocked at the sight, that I retired immediately with indignation and disgust — Suppose the matter of those ulcers, floating on the water, comes in contact with my skin, when the pores are all open, I would ask you what must be the consequence? — Good Heaven, the very thought makes my blood run cold!

...But I am now as much afraid of drinking, as of bathing; for after a long conversation with the Doctor, about the construction of the Pump and the cistern, it is very far from being clear with me, that the patients in the Pump-room don't swallow the scourings of the bathers. I can't help suspecting, that there is, or may be, some regurgitation from the bath into the cistern of the pump. In that case, what a delicate beveridge is every day quaffed by the drinkers; medicated with the sweat and dirt, and dandriff; and the abominable discharges of various kinds, from twenty different diseased bodies, parboiling in the kettle below. In order to avoid this filthy composition, I had recourse to the spring that supplies the private baths on the Abbey-Green; but I at once perceived something extraordinary in the taste and smell; and, upon inquiry, I find that the Roman baths in this quarter, were found covered by an old burying ground, belonging to the Abbey; thro' which, in all probability, the water drains in its passage: so that as we drink the decoction of living bodies at the Pump-room, we swallow the strainings of rotten bones and carcasses at the private bath — I vow to God, the very idea turns my stomach!

Humphrey Clinker
1771

JOHN WOOD

The Amusements Of Bath

The Amusements of *Bath* so insensibly engross the Time of the Stangers Resorting to the City, that nothing is more common than the graver sort of People to declare that they do nothing while they are at *Bath*, and yet can find no spare Time for the least Employ: Amusements so Sweet and Alluring must therefore be beyond the Power of a particular Description, even for the Space of a single Day, much less of a whole Year or a number of Years: So that from what I have already said, everybody must form their own Ideas of what necessarily passes between real and apparent People of Rank and Fortune when they Meet together in the Baths, Pump Rooms, Coffee Houses ...and other places of general Resort, as well as when they Meet in select Parties or on mutual Visits.

They may imagine all the different Scenes of Life to be Acting in this Theatre of the Polite World; and if I had that Turn of Thought which is necessary to form a compleat Novelist, I could enlarge this Chapter into a whole Volume, by relating the real Stories of Wit, Humour and Gallantry produced in any short Period of Time within the Memory of Man: I could point out the good and bad Fate of the Youth of both Sexes from their first Appearance in White Frocks, the real Emblems of their State of Innocence, till they, in the Years of their Maturity, attained the Summit of all Happiness, or sunk to the Root of all Misery, from well known Instances of but Yesterday's Date: and I could tell the Adventures of the Fortunate and Unfortunate, as well as of People under various other characters, in many remarkable Cases that have happened in the City since the Time I began to Improve it.

An Essay Towards a Description of Bath
1765

CHRISTOPHER ANSTEY

A Farewell To Bath

Paid bells, and musicians,
Drugs, nurse, and physicians,
Balls, raffles, subscriptions, and chairs;
Wigs, gowns, skins, and trimming,
Good books for the women,
Plays, concerts, tea, negus and prayers.

Paid the following schemes,
Of all who it seems
Make charity — bus'ness their care:
A gamester decay'd,
And a prudish old maid
By gaiety brought to despair;

A fiddler of note,
Who for lace on his coat,
To his taylor was much in arrears:
An author of merit,
Who wrote with such spirit
The pillory took off his ears.

...Farewell then, ye streams,
Ye poetical themes!
Swett fountains for curing the spleen!
I'm griev'd to the heart
Without cash to depart,
And quit this adorable scene!

Where gaming and grace
Each other embrace
Dissipation and piety meet
May all, who've a notion
Of cards or devotion,
make Bath their delightful retreat!

The New Bath Guide
1766

RICHARD SHERIDAN
The Ridotto Of Bath

At many grand Routs in my time I have been,
And many fine Rooms to be sure I have seen;
Al Fresco's, rich Gala's, Ridotto's and Balls,
From Carlisle's sweet palace to black City Halls;
From Almack's Long-Room to the Inn at Devizes,
From Birth-night eclat to the dance at Assizes:
All these I have serv'd at these twelve years and more,
Yet faith, I've seen here—what I ne'er saw before.
You'd like a description, I'm sure, my dear brother,
For fifty to one we mayn't have such another.

...At seven we opened and not very long
Before all the passages smoak'd with the throng;
All dress'd in their best — for Great Marshall WADE,
For fear the Coup d'Oiel should be darken'd by shade,
Had issued his orders to dizen the back,
With singular caution 'gainst wearing of black;
In gauds all must shine, he had given them warning,
Tho' the ghosts of their kindred should bellow for mourning;
Nay, more, this grand festival night to denote,
No creature must come with a cape to his coat,
Full trimm'd they should be, tho' a French frock would do,
But Officers must be in livery and queue:
And yet for all this, there were some so uncivil,
They came in their dolefuls as black as the Devil.

...But here I must mention the best thing of all,
And what I'm informed ever marks a Bath ball;
The VARIETY 'tis which so reign'd in the crew,
That turn where one would the classes were new;
For here no dull level of rank and degrees,
No uniform mode, that shews all are at ease;
But like a chess-table, part black and part white,
'Twas a delicate checker of low and polite.
The motley assemblage, so blended together,

'Twas Mob, or Ridotto, - 'twas both, or 'twas neither.

...But, - silence ye Hautboys! ye Fiddles be dumb!
Ye dancers stop instant - THE HOUR is come
The great! the all-wonderful hour - of EEATING!
That hour, - for which ye all know you've been waiting.
Well, the doors were unbolted, and in they all rush'd;
They crowded, they jostled, they jockey'd and push'd:
Thus at a Mayor's feast, a disorderly mob
Breaks in after dinner to plunder and rob.
I mean not by this to reflect on the gentry,
I'd only illustrate the *mode* of their *entry*;
For certain I am they meant no such foul play
But only were wishing to help us away.

...In files they march'd up to the sideboards, while each
Laid hands upon all the good things in his reach;
There stuck to his part, cramm'd while he was able,
And then carried off all he could from the table;
Our outworks they storm'd with prowess most manful,
And jellies and cakes carried off by the handful;
While some our lines enter'd with courage undaunted,
Nor quitted the trench 'till they'd got what they wanted.
...And thus in ten minutes one half of the treat
Made a pretty check carpet squash'd under their feet.
O 'twas pleasing to see a collection of beaux
Parading with large macarons at their toes,
Or a delicate nymph give a languishing reel
On a marmalade kissing her little French heel.
So you see, my dear *Hal*, they bore all things before 'em,
And trampled on *sweetmeats* as well as *decorum*.

Bath Chronicle
1771

FRANCES BURNEY
Bath, At The Right Season

The charming city of Bath answered all my expectations. The Crescent, the prospect from it, and the elegant symmetry of the Circus, delighted me. The Parades, I own, rather disappointed me; one of them is scarce preferable to some of the best paved streets in London, and the other, though it affords a beautiful prospect, a charming view of Prior Park and of the Avon, yet wanted something in *itself* of more striking elegance that a mere broad pavement, to satisfy the ideas I had formed of it.

At the pump-room, I was amazed at the public exhibition of the ladies in the bath: it is true, their heads are covered with bonnets, but the very idea of being seen, in such a situation, by whoever pleases to look, is indelicate.

"'Fore George," said the Captain, looking into the bath, "this would be a most excellent place for old Madame French to dance a fandango in! By Jingo, I wouldn't wish for better sport than to swing her round this here pond!"

"She would be very much obliged to you," said Lord Orville, "for so extraordinary a mark of your favour."

"Why, to let you know," answered the Captain, "she hit my fancy mightily; I never took so much to an old tabby before."

"Really, now," cried Mr. Lovel, looking also into the bath, "I must confess it is, to me, very incomprehensible why the ladies chuse that frightful unbecoming dress to bathe in! I have often pondered very seriously upon the subject, but could never hit upon the reason."

..."Pray, now," said the Captain, "did you ever get a ducking in that there place yourself?"

"A ducking, Sir!" repeated Mr. Lovel; "I protest I think that's rather an odd term! — but if you mean a *bathing*, it is an honour I have had many times."

...Mrs Beaumont then, addressing herself to Miss Mirvan and me, enquired how we liked Bath?

"I hope," said Mr. Lovel, "the Ladies do not call this *seeing Bath*."

"No! — what should ail 'em?" cried the Captain; "do you suppose they put their eyes in their pockets?"

"No, Sir; but I fancy you will find no person, — that is, no person of any condition, — call going about a places in a morning *see-ing Bath*."

"Mayhap, then," said the literal Captain, "you think then we should see it better by going about at midnight?"

"No, Sir, no," said Mr. Lovel, with a supercilious smile, "I perceive you don't understand me, — *we* should never call it *seeing Bath*, without going at the right season."

"Why, what a plague, then," demanded he, "can you only see at one season of the year?"

Mr. Lovel smiled again; but seemed superior to making any answer.

Evelina
1778

PHILLIP THICKNESSE
A New Prose Bath Guide

The very extraordinary and rapid increase of the city of BATH, within these last Twenty Years, both as to the Number and Quality of its Inhabitants, as well as the Extent of its Buildings, has been so great, that we question whether a Person well aquainted with this City Thirty Years ago, would be able to find out more than ONE MARK whereby he could ascertain its Originality; ...it is a MARK strongly pointed out by the Finger of God, as a Blessing to his Creatures; and therefore, while we are admiring the transitory Alteration made by Men, let us not neglect but admire ...that permanent Blessing, that Stream of Comfort which we know has flowed ...from the Beginning of Time; a Stream which pours forth Spirits to the dejected, Appetite to the depraved, and Strength to the emaciated: A Stream which may justly be called the Fountain of Life and the Cordial of the afflicted.

No Wonder then, if a Spot, so peculiarly favoured by Nature, surrounded by a beautiful and fertile Country, renowned for the Salubrity of its Air, as well as the Excellence of its Vegetable and Mineral Productions ...should become the constant Residence of a great Number of People of Fashion and Fortune.

For it is in BATH alone, where People of Fashion can step out of their Coaches after a long journey, into Houses or Lodgings, full as warm and as comfortable as their own and into many equally magnificent. It is in BATH alone where Men of every Age can, within a small Compass, and at little Expence, find such Amusements as are suitable to their Inclinations. The Men of Reading will find Libraries always open to them; the Men of Conversation, a Variety of Company to form an agreeable Party with. To the Gay and Youthful of both sexes, it is a Paradise; to Men in Years, a most comfortable Retreat.

The New Prose Bath Guide
1778

No ties can hold him, no affection bind;
And Fear alone restrains his Coward mind:
Free him from that no monster is so fell,
Nor is so sure a Bloodhound found in hell.

PHILIP THICKNESSE Esq.ʳ

FRANZ J HADYN

A Note On Bath

On the 2nd of August 1794. I left London for Bath and arrived at 8 o' clock in the evening. I lived at the house of Herr Rauzzini a musicus who is very famous, and who in his time was one of the greatest singers. He is a very nice and hospitable man.

Bath is one of the most beautiful cities in Europe. All the houses are built of stone; this stone comes from quarries in the surrounding mountains; it is very white. The whole city lies on a slope and that is why there are very few carriages: instead of them there are a lot of sedan-chairs, who will take you quite a way for six-pence. But too bad that there are so few straight roads; there are a lot of beautiful squares, on which stand the most magnificent houses, but which cannot be reached by any vehicle.

Today, on the 3rd, I looked at the city, and found, half-way up the hill, a building shaped like a half-moon and more magnificent than any I had seen in London. The curve extends for 100 fathoms and there is a corinthian column at each fathom.

The city is not thickly populated, and in the Summer one sees very few people; for the people taking the baths don't come till the beginning of October, and stay through half of February. The baths by nature are very warm; one bathes in the water, and one always drinks it — generally better the latter.

I made the aqaintance there of Miss Brown, a charming person of the best conduit; a good piano-forte player, her mother a most beautiful woman. The city is now building a most spendid room for guests taking the cure.

Notebook
1794

MR KNIGHT

A Ramble To Bath

Up and down, round about all the streets I paraded,
And seed Beaux who didn't know their beauties was invaded.
Their coats were so cut away .... breeches to expose,
And heads so beshrivll'd up .... cordles covered half their nose.

Then the ladies so dress, they do bury all their chin,
So lac'd in the middle to look taper and thin.
While behind, hoops and all, they do need nothing more
But weight enow to balance what they carry here afore.

How I laughed O my sides, to see some ladies walking,
All about fast asleep, and whats more they was talking.
But in a dream I suppose, for all around about their heads,
The curtains were drawn just as tho' they were in bed.

In the Crescent, 'tis as fine a place ever I did see,
The Beaux shorten pace with Belles to agree.
Niddle noodle, to and fro, and to view each that passes,
For fear their eyes should wear out, they do stare thro' looking
glasses.

In the Pump room full crammed ... 'tis a sight for to see,
And stranger to tell, there all ranks do agree,
For like corks in a box, stuck up right cheek by jole,
Push but one and bob ... goes the body of the whole.

But what pleased I most was to see in fine weather,
Fine folk ride about in them things made of leather.
While two men with long poles ... all the world like a bier
Trot along with the corpse ... stuck an end in the air.

At last having seed all the sights and fine places
Sops, baths, rooms, parades and a sight of strange faces
I thought I'd come here tho' my tale made ye laugh
To tell ye this sight pleases I the best by half.

Jacobs Return from London
1789

SIR WALTER SCOTT
Childhood Recollections At Bath

I was in my fourth year when my father was advised that the Bath waters might be of some advantage to my lameness. My affectionate aunt, although such a journey promised to a person of her retired habits anything but pleasure or amusement, undertook as readily to accompany me to the wells of Bladud, as if she had expected all the delight that ever the prospect of a watering-place held out to its most impatient visitants.

...At Bath, where I lived about a year, I went through all the usual discipline of the pump-room and baths, but I believe without the least advantage to my lameness. ... In other respects my residence at Bath is marked by very pleasing recollections ... I never recall them without a feeling of pleasure. The beauties of the parade (which of them I know not), with the river Avon winding around it, and the lowing of the cattle from the opposite hills, are warm in my recollection, and are only rivalled by the splendours of a toy shop somewhere near the Orange Grove. I had acquired, I know not by what means, a kind of superstitious terror for statuary of all kinds. No ancient Iconoclast or modern Calvinist could have looked on the outside of the Abbey church ... with more horror than the image of Jacob's Ladder, with all its angels, presented to my infant eye. My uncle effectually combatted my terrors, and formally introduced me to a statue of Neptune, which perhaps still keeps guard at the side of the Avon, where a pleasure boat crosses to Spring Gardens.

After being a year at Bath, I returned to Edinburgh, and afterwards for a season to Sandy-Knowe; where it was thought sea-bathing might be of service to my lameness.

Memoir of his Early Years
1808

JOHN CAM HOBHOUSE
Snug Lying

It sound rather strange, but I tell you no lie,
There's many good people that come here to die;
For the London practitioners wisely declare,
When their patients can't breathe, they must try change of air.
Says Sir Walter — "Dear Lady, I thought all the while,"
"That dropsy of your's must proceed from the bile;"
"The waters of Bath have made wonderful cures"
"Of many I know, in such cases as your's,"
"You'll go down directly to Bath if you're wise." —
So down goes my Lady directly — and dies —
"To tell her the truth of the case would have shock'd her,"
"But , thank heav'n, she's off of my hands," — says the doctor.
...These folk, like Sir Lucius, find comfort in dying,
Because in the Abbey there's very snug lying
Or like to be carried in pickle and salt,
A hundred long miles to the family vault;
Else, why should they leave all their comforts, and come
To die in a lodging so distant from home?
Such cases are frequent, and yet not a few
Come here to be ill, just for something to do.
Then, too, we've the nervous, as David observes,
What would come of the doctors, except for the nerves?
These delicate creatures, they feel no aversion
To join the rest in gen'ral diversion.
Each morning the medical gentleman calls,
Each evening my Lady stands up at the balls:
What with parties and routs, 'ere the season is ended,
At last she becomes what at first she pretended:
There was young Fanny Fashion, poor creature! sent out
Some dozens of cards for a supper and rout:—
"Mrs Fashion at home — Tuesday next — a small party — "
"And, thanks for inquiries, she finds herself hearty;"
But Pluto, alas! without half so much warning,
Invited her down to a party that morning.
That very same evening I happen'd to dine,
With dear Lady G....; she's a fav'rite of mine;

Her carriage was full, but she gave me a lift,
For I sat all the way in her lap for a shift;
So driving along, when we came to the door,
A footman stepp'd up — "Sir, my Lady's no more!" —
"What dead? O dear me! what a horrible thing!"
"What dead!" said her Ladyship, pulling the string,
"'Tis dreadfully shocking — I hope she's in heav'n."
"Here, coachman, drive down to number eleven."

Wonders of a Week at Bath
1811

ROBERT SOUTHEY

A Letter From Bath

If other cities are interesting as being old, Bath is not less so being new. It has no aqueduct, no palaces, no gates, castle, or city walls, yet it is the finest and most striking town I have ever seen
   ...I passed the whole morning in perambulating the town, seeing it in all its parts. The cathedral is small but beautiful. ... The pump-room is a handsome building, and bears above the entrance the words of Pindar, 'Water is Best' here used in a sense concerning which there can be no dispute. ... There are two public ball-rooms, and two masters of the ceremonies, Beau Nash's empire having been divided, because it was grown too large for the superintendence of any individual. ... Some sober Englishmen in the anti-chambers were silently busied at whist, though it was noon day, — some of them, it seems, make it the study of their lives and others their trade. It is a fine place for gamblers and for that species of men called fortune-hunters, a race of swindlers of the worst kind, who are happily unknown in Spain. They make it their business to get a wife of fortune, having none themselves: age, ugliness and even idiocy, being no objections.
...It also the Canaan of Physicians; for it abounds with wealthly patients, many of whom will have any disease which the doctor will be pleased to find out for them: but even Canaan may be overstocked, and, it seems, more of Death's advanced guard have assembled here than can find milk and honey.

Letters from England
1803

LOUIS SIMOND

A Brief Sojourn At Bath

We arrived at Bath last night. The chaise drew up in style at the White Hart. Two well-dressed footmen were ready to help us to alight, presenting an arm on each side. Then a loud bell on the stairs, and lights carried before us to an elegantly furnished sitting room, where the fire was already blazing. In a few minutes, a neat-looking chambermaid, with an ample white apron, pinned behind, came to offer her services to the ladies, and shew the bedrooms. In less than half an hour, five powdered *gentlemen* burst into the room with three dishes etc and two remained to wait. I give this as a sample of the best, or rather of the finest inns. Our bill was £2.11 sterling, dinner for three, tea, beds and breakfast. The servants have no wages, — but, depending on the generosity of travellers they find it their interest to please them. They (the servants) cost us about five shillings a day.

This morning we have explored the town, which is certainly very beautiful. It is built of freestone, of a fine cream-colour, and contains several public edifices, in a good taste. We remarked a circular place called the Crescent, another called the Circus; — all the streets straight and regular. This town looks as if it had been cast in a mould all at once; so new, so fresh and regular. The building where the medical water is drank, and where the baths are, exhibits very different objects; human nature, old, infirm and in ruins, or weary and *ennuyé*. Bath is a sort of great monastery, inhabited by single people, particularly superannuated females. No trade, no manufactures, no occupations of any sort, except that of killing time, the most laborious of all. Half of the inhabitants do nothing, the other half supply them with nothings: — Multitude of splendid shops, full of all that wealth and luxury can desire, arranged with all the arts of seduction.

Being in haste and not equipped for the place, we left it at three o' clock.

Journal of a Tour & Residence in Great Britain
1810/1811

JANE AUSTEN

A New Aquaintance at Bath

Every morning now brought its regular duties; — shops were to be visited; some new part of the town to be looked at; and the Pump-room to be attended, where they paraded up and down for an hour, looking at every body and speaking to no one. The wish of a numerous aquaintance in Bath was still uppermost with Mrs. Allen, and she repeated it after every fresh proof, which every morning brought, of her knowing nobody at all.

They made they appearance in the Lower Rooms; and here fortune was more favourable to our heroine. The master of the ceremonies introduced to her a very gentle-manlike young man as a partner; — his name was Tilney. He seemed to be about four or five and twenty, was rather tall, had a pleasing countenance, a very intelligent and lively eye, and, if not quite handsome, was very near it. His address was good, and Catherine felt herself in high luck. There was little leisure for speaking while they danced; but when they were seated for tea, she found him as agreeable as she had already given him credit for being. After chatting some time on such matters as naturally arose from the objects around them, he suddenly addressed her with — "Have you been long in Bath, madam?"

"About a week, sir," replied Catherine, trying not to laugh.

"Really!" with affected astonishment.

"Why should you be surprized, sir?"

"Why, indeed?" said he, in his natural tone — 'but some emotion must appear to be raised by your reply, and surprize is more easily assumed, and not less reasonable than any other. — Now let us go on. Were you never here before madam?"

"Never, sir."

"Indeed! Have you yet honoured the Upper Rooms?"

"Yes, sir, I was there last Monday."

"Have you been to the theatre?"

"Yes, sir, I was at the play on Tuesday."

"To the concert?"

'Yes, sir, on Wednesday."

"And are you altogether pleased with Bath?"

"Yes — I like it very well."

"Now I must give one smirk, and then we may be rationable again."

Northanger Abbey 1818

A.B. GRANVILLE
Approach and Arrival at Bath

As we approached the city nearer and nearer coming from the south, a sight burst suddenly upon me the effect of which seemed as if produced by one of those magic representations of a night scene introduced into French ballets, where, in the midst of darkness, hundreds of enchanted palaces appear one placed higher than another, until the highest seem to touch the dark azure vault, and, with their glittering casement-lights, mock the dazzling stars of heaven. The twinkling of all the gas-lights, too, profusely arranged in front of the many terraced edifices and crescents placed on different hills and alone visible, while the buildings themselves were just distinguishable in the shadow of night; and the splendour thrown over the streets nearest to the steep road, down which we rapidly descended into the town, passing, at the same time, under the great Gothic arch that supports the Great Western Railway, to enter Southgate-street, — all these things combined presented to my mind a scene unequalled in any city.

...From whichever point, either of the old or the new city, we cast our glance around, a height, an eminence, or a hill presents itself with its own peculiar beauties, natural and acquired. Being all of them, parts of a great oolitic range, their shapes are gracefully rounded or waving: and whether we track the steep ascent of CLAVERTON... or ...the loftier range... called LANSDOWN HILL, ...we find every part of the horizon occupied by some picturesque rising in the land, once barren and almost inaccessible, but now of easy access and teeming with a busy population.

Spas of England
1841

WILLIAM M THACKERAY
As For Bath

As for Bath, all history went and bathed and drank there. George II and his Queen, Prince Frederick and his Court, scarce a character one can mention of the early last century but was seen in that famous Pump Room where Beau Nash presided, and his picture hung between the busts of Newton and Pope:

> "This picture placed these busts between
> Gives satire all its strength:
> Wisdom and Wit are little seen
> But Folly at full length"

I should like to have seen the Folly. It was a splendid embroidered, beruffled, snuff-boxed, red-heeled impertinent Folly, and knew how to make itself repected. I should like to have seen that noble mad-cap Peterborough in his boots (he actually had the audacity to walk about Bath in boots!), with his blue ribbon and stars, and a cabbage under each arm, and a chicken in his hand, which he had been cheapening for his dinner. Chesterfield came there many a time and gambled for hundreds, and grinned through his gout. Mary Wortley (Montegu) was there, young and beautiful; and Mary Wortley old, hideous, and snuffy. Miss Chudleigh came there, slipping away from one husband, and on the look-out for another. Walpole passed many a day there, sickly, supercilious, absurdly dandified, and affected; with a brilliant wit, a delightful sensibility; and for his friends a most tender, generous, and faithful heart. And if you and I had been alive then, and strolling down Milsom Street — hush! we should have taken our hats off, as an awful, long, lean, gaunt figure, swathed in flannels passed by in its chair, and a livid face looked out from the window — great fierce eyes staring from under a bushy powdered wig, a terrible frown, a terrible Roman nose — and we whisper to one another. "There he is! There's the great commoner! There is Mr. Pitt!" As we walk away the abbey bells are set a-ringing; and we meet our testy friend Toby Smollett on the arm of James Quinn the actor.

The Four Georges
1857

CHARLES DICKENS
The Waters

"Perhaps we had better be walking," said Mr Smauker, consulting a copper time-piece which dwelt at the bottom of a deep watch-pocket, and was raised to the surface by means of a black string, with a copper key at the other end.

"P'raps we had," replied Sam, "or they'll overdo the swarry, and that'll spile it."

"Have you drank the waters, Mr Weller?" inquired his companion, as they walked towards High Street.

"Once," replied Sam.

"What did you think of 'em, Sir?"

"I thought they was particklery unpleasant," replied Sam.

"Ah,"said Mr John Smauker, "you disliked the killibeate taste, perhaps?"

"I don't know much about that 'ere," said Sam. "I thought they'd a wery strong flavour o' warm flat irons."

"That IS the killibeate, Mr Weller," observed Mr John Smauker, contemptuously.

"Well, if it is, it's a wery inexpressive word, that's all," said Sam. "It may be, but I ain't much in the chemical line myself, so I can't say." And here, to the great horror of Mr John Smauker, Sam Weller began to whistle.

The Pickwick Papers
1836

CHARLES TENNYSON TURNER

The Two Eras

In that old pump-room, as I stood alone
Beside the Bath, the old waters of the sun,
I thought of two past eras: All were gone
To evening haunts of pleasure and of fun,
As they went off to dine, and dance, and sup,
The Bath began to teem with modish ghosts,
A reach of Lethe, sending bubbles up
From bygone dandies, and forgotten toasts.
Then, for relief, I turn'd to see and hear
An older past, with fancy's eye, that takes
Fond retrospects, and fancy's ear, that makes
A sound of her own longings. Ofttimes here
A home and grave the peaceful Roman found
And little Caius coo'd on British ground.

Sonnets
1873

ANTHONY TROLLOPE
Fashionable Lodgings

I fear that Miss Mackenzie, when she betook herself to Littlebath, had before mind's eye no sufficiently settled plan of life. She wished to live pleasantly and perhaps fashionably; but she also desired to live respectably and with due regard to religion. How she was to set about doing this at Littlebath, I am afraid she did not quite know.

She had indeed been induced to migrate from London to Littlebath by an accident which should not have been allowed to actuate her. She had been ill, and the doctor with that solicitude which doctors sometime feel for ladies who are not well to do in the world, had recommended change of air. Littlebath, among the Tantivy hills, would be the very place for her. There were waters at Littlebath which she might drink for a month or two with great advantage to her system. It was then the end of July, and anybody who was everybody was going out of town. Suppose she were to go to Littlebath in August, and stay there for a month, or perhaps two months, as she might feel inclined.

She made a preliminary journey to that place, and took furnished lodgings in the Paragon. Now it is know to all the world that the Paragon is the nucleus of all this is pleasant and fashionable in Littlebath. It is a long row of houses whith two short rows abutting from the ends of the long row, and every house in it looks out upon the Montpellier Gardens. If not built of stone, these houses are built of such stucco that the Margret Mackenzie's of the world do not know the difference. Six steps which are of undoubted stone lead up to each door. The areas are grand with high railings. The flagged way before the houses is very broad, and at each corner there is an extensive sweep so that the carriages of the Paragonites may be made to turn easily.

Miss Mackenzie
1865

REVEREND F KILVERT
Prior Park

Thursday 22 January 1874

I went to Bath this morning by the 11'o'clock train to stay at Upland Villa with the Gwatkinses till Saturday. Upland Villa is high upon Bathwick Hill above Claverton Lodge.

In the afternoon Mr. Gwatkin, Annie and I walked through Widcombe by the ivied Church under Crow Hall and up the private road to Prior Park. We went boldly in at the lodge Gates and made our way unchallenged past the long damp dreary ranges of ugly buildings, half barrack, half jail, till we turned the last wing and came round to the garden front and the great portico looking over Bath. The shrubbery... overgrown with long neglect. Upon the great stone balustrades of the wide terrace stairs sat four peacocks, one a white bird, a huge white swan lumbered waddling along a grass-grown gravel path on his way down to the lakes in the hollow of the park, and two ecclesiastics in cassocks and birettas tramped up and down the grand terrace-walk smoking, laughing and spitting right and left. Every now and then the strange musical note of a swan sounded like a trumpet from the bushes. Splendid terraces with balustrades of carved stone and broad shallow flights of stone steps descended from the great portico to the lawns and gardens and the distant lakes gleaming misty in the wooded hollow.

From the vast portico where Pope, Allen and Warburton used to sit and talk the view over Bath and the beautiful valley is said to be glorious on a fine summer evening at sunset and I can quite believe it. This afternoon the weather was unfortunately foggy and the Abbey Tower could only just be faintly discerned looming through the mist.

The Diary of Francis Kilvert
1874

THOMAS HARDY
A True Blot in Bath

Directly Cain mentioned Bath, they all threw down their hooks and forks and drew round him.

…"Yes, " he continued, directing his thoughts to Bath and letting his eyes follow, "I've seed the world at last — yes — and I've seed our mis'ess — ahok-hok-hok!"

"Bother the boy!" said Gabriel. "Something is always going the wrong way down your throat, so you can't tell what's necessary to be told."

…"Now then," said Gabriel impatiently, "what did you see, Cain?"

"I seed our mis'ess go into a sort of park place, where there's seats, and shrubs and flowers, arm-in-crook with a sojer," continued Cainy firmly…

Gabriel's features seem to get thinner. "Well, what did you see besides?"

"Oh, all sorts."

"White as a lily? You are sure 'twas she?"

"Yes."

"Well, what besides?"

"Great glass windows to the shops, and great clouds in the sky, full of rain, and wooden trees in the country round."

"You stun-poll! What will ye say next?" said Coggan.

"Let en alone," interposed Joseph Poorgrass. "The boy's maning is that the sky and the earth in the kingdom of Bath is not altogether different from ours here. 'Tis for our good to gain knowledge of strange cities, and as such the boy's words should be suffered, so to speak it."

"And the people of Bath," continued Cain, "never need to light their fires except as a luxury, for the water springs up out of the earth ready boiled for use."

"'Tis true as the light," testified Matthew Moon. "I've hear other navigators say the same thing.

"They drink nothing else there," said Cain, "and seem to enjoy it, to see how they swaller it down."

"Well, it seem a barbarian practice enough to us, but I daresay the natives think nothing o' it," said Matthew.

97

"And don't victuals spring up as well as drink?" asked Coggan, twirling his eye.

"No — I own to a blot there in Bath — a time blot. God didn't provide 'em with victuals as well as drink, and 'twas a drawback I couldn't get over at all."

"Well, 'tis a curious place, to say the least," observed Moon: "and it must be a curious people that live therein."

Far From The Madding Crowd
1874

ALGERNON CHARLES SWINBURNE

A Ballad of Bath

Like a queen enchanted who may not laugh, or weep,
    Glad at heart and guarded from change and care like ours,
Girt about with beauty by days and nights that creep
    Soft as breathless ripples that softly shoreward sweep,
Lies the lovely city whose grace no grief deflowers.
    Age and grey forgetfulness, time that shifts and veers,
Touch not thee, our fairest whose charm no rival nears,
    Hailed as England's Florence of one whose praise gives

                                      grace,
Landor, once thy lover, a name that love reveres:
    Dawn and noon and sunset are one before thy face.

Dawn whereof we know not and noon whose fruit we reap,
    Garnered up in record of years that fell like flowers,
Sunset like sunrise along the shining steep
    Whence thy fair face lightens, and where thy soft springs

                                       leap,
Crown at once and gird thee with grace of guardian powers.
    Loved of men beloved of us, souls that fame inspheres,
All thine air hath music for him who dreams and hears;
    Voices mixed of multitudes, feet of friends that pace,
Witness why for ever, if heaven's face clouds or clears,
    Dawn and noon and sunset are one before thy face.

Peace hath here found harbourage mild as very sleep:
    Not the hills and waters, the fields and wildwood bowers,
Smile or speak more tenderly, clothed with peace more deep,
    Here than memory whispers of day our memories keep
Fast with love and laughter dreams of withered hours.
    Bright were these blossom of old, and thought endears
Still the fair soft phantoms that pass with smiles or tears,
    Sweet as roseleaves hoarded and dired wherein we trace
Still the soul and spirit of sense that lives and cheers:
    Dawn and noon and sunset are one before thy face.
City lulled asleep by the chime of passing years,
    Sweeter smiles thy rest than the radiance round they peers;
Only love and lovely rememberance here have place.
    Time on thee lies lighter than music and men's ears;
Dawn and noon and sunset are one before thy face.

1870

BOOTH TARKINGTON
The King of Bath

Beau Nash stood at the door of the Rooms smiling blandly upon a dainty throng in the pink of its finery and gay furbelows. The great exquisite bent his body constantly in a series of consummately adjusted bows: before a great dowager, seeming to sweep the floor in august deference; somewhat stately to the young bucks; greeting the wits with gracious friendliness and a twinkle of raillery; inclining with fatherly gallantry before the beauties; the degree of his inclination measured the altitude of the recipient as accurately as a nicely calculated sand-glass measures the hours.

The King of Bath was happy, for wit, beauty, fashion — to speak more concretely: nobles, belles, gamesters, beaux, statesmen and poets — made fairyland (or opera bouffe, at least) in his dominions; play ran higher and higher, and Mr. Nash's coffers filled up with gold. To crown his pleasure, a prince of the French blood, the young Comte de Beaujolais, just arrived from Paris, had reached Bath at noon in state, accompanied by the Marquis de Mirepoix, the ambassador of Louis XV. The Beau dearly prized the society of the lofty, and the present visit was an honour to Bath: hence to the Master of Ceremonies. What was better, there would be some profitable hours with cards and dice.

So it was that Mr. Nash smiled never more benignly than on that bright evening. The Rooms rang with the silvery voices of women and delightful laughter, while the fiddles went merrily, their melodies chiming sweetly with the joyance of his mood.

Monsieur Beaucaire
1900

HENRY CHAPPELL

Queen Bath

Shrine of the healing waters, peerless Bath,
   Gem in meet setting of the mighty hills,
Whose rugged breasts, by many a devious path,
   Pour in benificence thy God-blest rills.

Majestic city, thy time-hallowed walls
   Are fraught with memories of thy mighty dead;
Art, letters, arms, each marble pale recalls—
   The fire of genius, all diversely spread.

Herein, the mighty Roman hand hath wrought
   An inner shrine, and carved with cunning steel
Palatial baths, for those who healing sought,
   And they who feared the ills they did not feel.

Here are the wonders of Italia's art
   Epitomized, discovered to the eye.
Wrest from confusion's self, a noble part
   Stands here to speak of ancient symmetry.

Cornice and column, adamantine wall,
   Alters and friezes, while from sacred place
The mortal Gorgon's eyes upon us fall
   From out the writhing serpent's chill embrace.

Despite Time's wasting passage, still it bears
   Weird beauty, half barbaric, all its own,
As when the sculptor in the far off years
   Tortured a soul-less block to living stone.

The Day and other Poems
1918

THOMAS HARDY
Aquae Sulis

The chimes called midnight, just at interlune,
And the daytime parle on the Roman investigations
Was shut to silence, save for the husky tune
The bubbling waters played near the excavations.

And a warm air came up from underground,
And the flutter of a filmy shape unsepulchred,
That collected itself, and waited, and looked around:
Nothing was seen, but utterances could be heard:

Those of the Goddess whose shrine was beneath the pile
Of the God with the baldachined altar overhead:
"And what did you win by raising this nave and aisle
Close on the site of the temple I tenanted?

"The notes of your organ have thrilled down out of view
To the earth-clogged wrecks of my edifice many a year,
Though stately and shining once — ay, long ere you
Had set up crucifix and candle here.

"Your priests have trampled the dust of mine without rueing,
Despising the joys of man whom I so much loved,
Though my springs boil on by your Gothic arcades and
pewing,
And sculptures crude ...... Would Jove they could be removed!'

"Repress, O lady proud, your traditional ires;
You know not by what a frail thread we equally hang;
It is said we are images both — twitched by people's desires:
And that I, as you, fail like a song men yesterday sang!"

"What — a Jumping-jack you, and myself but a poor Jumping-
jill,
Now worm-eaten, times agone twitched at Humanity's bid?
O I cannot endure it! — But, chance to us whatso there will,
Let us kiss and be friends! Come, agree you?" — None heard if
he did....

And the olden dark hid the cavities late laid bare,
And all was suspended and soundless as before,
Except for a gossamery noise fading off in the air,
And the boiling voice of the waters' medicinal pour.

Satires of Circumstance
1890

G K CHESTERTON

On Bath

I happen to have been wandering about in the ancient and modern city of Bath. As it happens, it is in a rather special sense ancient and modern; it is not in a visible sense very medieval. Those correspondents who imagine that I am never happy except when embracing a gargoyle or enacting the ceremonial of a guild would picture me as forlorn in a place so classical; but I am feeling very cheerful, thank you. Bath is indeed associated with one grand gargoyle as great as a catherdral. The wife of Bath is a figure as formidable as Mrs Gamp, and conceived in truth with greater charity than that of Charles Dickens. But, in the main, Bath is, as I have said, a city of the Romans and of the rationalist eigthteenth century, with something of a valley of oblivion in between. Yet I do not sit down and weep by the waters of Bath as by the waters of Babylon, or hang my medieval harp on eighteenth-century popular.

...The truth is that I, for one, feel a great sympathy not only for the place, but for the period. I do not say that I model myself on Beau Nash in every detail of dress and demeanour, but I pick up with great interest all the stories about him, and all that was typical of his time.

Generally Speaking
1928

H V MORTON

I Sink Into Bath

I have decided that when I grow old, with or without gout, sciatica, rheumatisim, or lumbago, I will retire on Bath with an ebony cane and a monocle. I like Bath: it has quality. I like Bath buns, Bath Olivers, Bath chaps, Bath brick and Bath stone and few sights are more stimulating to relaxed nerves than to sit on the hotel terrace opposite the Pump Room and watch the Bath chairs dash past. We were often told in the army that the speed of Bath is that of its slowest chair. Some months ago the local paper reported that a woman was run over by a Bath chair. That is the great danger here. As long as you can keep awake you may survive.

The crowds in Bath move slowly. Noises here are alouder than anywhere else on earth. A motor-cycle coming up Stall Street sounds like a giant rattling Cleopatra's Needle along the area railings vast as oak trees. Bath was made for chairs. Sedan and the other kind. Anything else on wheels is a rude invasion. One of the most soothing sights in England is the vista through the black Georgian pillars in Stall street — the Pump Room to the right, the lovely Abbey in the background, the foreground occupied by the Bath chairmen in various peaceful attitudes.

On wet days the chairmen sleep inside their chairs with little doors closed, sitting up behind glass panels like mummies in their sarcophagi; on fine days they sleep outside them.

"Your profession is not an exciting one?" I suggested to a veteran chairman.

He considered for some time and replied:

"No"

"I can't think how you all make a living out of Bath chairs,"

"We don't. We do a little carpet-beating now and then and odd jobs. It isn't much of a life."

In Search of England
1927

H G WELLS

Bath By Moonlight

They came into the town through unattractive and unworthy out-skirts, and only realised the charm of the place after they had garaged their car at the Pulteney Hotel and walked back over the Pulteney Bridge to see the Avon and the Pump Room and the Roman Baths. The Pulteney they found hung with pictures and adorned with sculpture to an astonishing extent: ...with white marble fauns and sylphs and lions and Ceasars and Queen Victorias... packed like an exhibition ...admist which splendours a competent staff ad-ministers modern comforts with an old-fashioned civility. But round and about the Pulteney one has still the scenery of Georgian England, the white faintly classical terraces and houses of the days of Fielding, Smollett, Fanny Burney and Jane Austen, the graceful bridge with the bright little shops ful of 'presents from Bath'; the Pump Room with its water drinkers and a fine array of the original Bath chairs.

In the afternoon Miss Seyffert came with Sir Richmond and Miss Grammont and was very enthusiastic about everything, but in the evening after dinner, it was clear that her role was to remain in the hotel. Sir Richard and Miss Grammont went out into the moonlit gloaming; they crossed the bridge again and followed the road beside the river towards the Old Abbey Church, that Lantern of the West. Away in some sunken gardens ahead of them a band was playing, and a cluster of little lights about the bandstand showed a crowd of people down below dancing on the grass. These little lights, these bobbing black heads and the lilting music ...made the dome of the moonlit world world about it seem very vast and cool and silent. Our visitors began to realise that Bath could be very beautiful. They went to the parapet above the river and stood there leaning over it elbow to elbow and smoking cigarettes. Miss Gram-mont was moved to declare the Pulteney Bridge with its noble arch, its effect of height over the swirling river, and cluster of houses above, more beautiful than the Ponte Vecchio at Florence. Down below was a man in waders with a fishing-rod going to and fro along the foaming weir, and a couple of boys paddled a boat against the rush of the water lower down the stream

Secret Places of the Heart
1933

H M BATEMAN

Bath, Past And Present

For anyone beginning an English tour there could hardly be a better town in which to start than Bath. Solid, cosy, well-to-do, and "correct", it seems to sum up the British ideal. Nothing jars here. Everything is mellow, toned down to a discreet delicacy. Even the Bath buns, in this their home town, are less formidable than others of the same denomination which one encounters in tea shops over the country.

It is an old place in every sense of the word, from the age of its foundation to the average age of the people one see walking, or being borne, upon its streets. It may even be described as a Temple of Antiquity. There are more antique shops to the hundred yards here than I know of in any other town in England. It is just the place in which to run earth that piece of old silver you have been hunting all through your life, or to aquire the nice little specimens of bric-a-brac that warm the cockles of your discriminating heart.

And all this has been done on water; water of the politest and most discreet kind imaginable.

"I'm afraid it will be very objectionable." I overheard a lady saying as she entered the Grand Pump Room, obviously for the first time in her life, intent upon drinking some of the water.

"Not at all, madam." the uniformed attendent reassured her. "It is a little warm and has a slight taste; that is all."

And so it is. That's just like Bath. Neither too hot nor too cold and with just enough flavour to make it interesting and to foster the idea of a cure. Indeed, if your doctor in prescribing a course of waters for you says it is to be taken at Bath, you are to be congratulated.

What could be more pleasant and soothing for the aged, or delicate, than to enter this impeccable Pump Room, receive the daily quota of water from the hands of a purple-clad damsel, and to sip it, sitting meanwhile upon a Sheraton settee, perusing the current illustrated journals, or perhaps dealing with one's correspondence at one of the writing tables so thoughtfully provided.

Bath Past and Present
1939

ANONYMOUS

Elevenses

Although it's a whole-time, nay, an overtime job
Ridding the earth of Mr Shicklemebob,
Although our world is all at sixes and sevens,
There'll always be an "elevenses".
Here in this city where sparkling waters run
And the Roman tub is less revered than the bun
(Lord Woolton must have his fun) —
Here, if we're able
To snatch a table,
Let's sit and, thanks to a bountiful bean,
Survey the scene.
Useless to call or beckon or even whistle a waiter;
We are the waiters now, he the dictator.
Dotted around are elderly hearties and smarties
Giving their coffee parties;
Grimly, gaily and daily
Holding the fort,
Whatever the ration report
Or the latest pranks of "that man".
Here are evacuees, blitzees and billetees,
An obvious Monte, a patent Le Touquet, a palpable Cannes —
Some that have travelled by Blue Train,
Others by Crewe train —
Men from the Services, Foam-guards and Home-guards, civilian
officials,
ATSies and WAAFies and other go-to-it initials;
Here is a bevy of beaty-tomorrow perhaps they'll be
"Bevinses"—
Meanwhile, there's "elevenses";
And over there in the corner (fifth table up),
Sipping a garrulous cup,
Nibbling a bellicose bun
Sits Public War-Wager Number One —
The genesis
(So it is whispered) of Menaces.
The air boils with the bubbling vibrations

Of innumerable confabulations,
Against which a full-blooded Strauss
Steals from the radio like a mouse.
Let's see if we can't get a slant
On the hubbub; that clever-faced woman in blue
(Next table) may give us a clue —
The one who is deep in a chat
With that dame in a bombed-looking hat.
Let's hitch up our hearing a peg........
"My dear, what I love is an EGG."

Punch 1941

BATH. JULIAN ROAD 29 4 42

110

CHARLES WHITBY

The Bombed City. May 1942

A war-proved veteran is Bath today,
Her churches burnt or blasted, homesteads felled
    And those Palladian Rooms whose grace compelled
World-homage, alas, bleak portents of dismay!
At every turn, in hideous disarray,
    Vistas of desolation are beheld.
    Wounded, but still majestic, still unquelled,
O City, a brutal horde has passed this way!

They came, they loosed their loads, leaving behind
As emblems of their Chief's distorted mind
    Insensate havoc and slaughter. Futile crime!
Adding to Bath's long blazon of renown
These last and brightest jewels of her crown,
    Courage indomitable and faith sublime.

In Yeovil Town
1947

WRENNE JARMAN

Bath

Fed by the mothering Mendips, this stone city:
A blackened miniature under bleaker skies
Of white Palladian sires. A latin quality,
An accent never lost, about it lies.

Here lies a royal body, incorrupt,
Through the thick glass of Time, the smile it wears
Is tranquil as in life: nothing abrupt
Has closed its understanding with the years.

The years go over its features with lovingness.
The Avon swans with love caress the river:
The Abbey Jesus looks down only to bless:
The turret Angels embrace their ladders forever.

Forever, like fond parents trained to note
The least noise in the night, we, listening long
And with a contrite heart, can isolate
Stone's timber's iron's, a building's, a city's song.

The song of this stone city is plain-chant,
Rising and falling in a susuration
Continuous, untiring — and intolerant
Of single hymns as of the generations.

The generations hear from their worn tombs.
Their effigies in the grey flesh of their city
Lie with stiff, folded hands awaiting Doom,
And an appeased Medusa's quickening pity.

Poetry Quarterly
1945

ALISTAIR COOKE

A Letter From Bath

Reflection on the City and Frank Lloyd Wright

I knew there was some link between my guilty feeling on entering
Bath and this plaguey memory of Frank Lloyd Wright. I looked at
Bath, as I had done three or four years ago, and in defiance of the
old master, I dare say it is a beautiful town to look on and soon
will be lovelier still. This is because the City of Bath, like so many
other places in Britain, had to suffer the scare and destruction of
a bombing or two to appreciate the noble things it had for so long
allowed to run down. The first time I was in Bath after the war,
the Roman baths, the great Abbey, the crescents built by John Wood
and his son were black with grime and pitted with rot. In the last
year or two Bath has wakened up with a bang to what is unique
about its heritage: an eighteenth century town built in a single style
out of local stone that abounds in nearby quarries. As they have
done in so many other old towns of England, in Cambridge most
wonderfully of all, they have blasted away the centuries of dirt that
had added more grime than bloom, and today you can see the two
great crescents and the Circus as they were in the seventeen-sixties
and -seventies. Great lyrical arcs of a light biscuit colour, gay and
graceful as they were meant to be.

...The Abbey no longer sits there like a lumpish Gothic tomb.
It shimmers in the late afternoon light, and on the west front one
can now see teams of angels having a rollicking time rushing up
and down (I don't know why down) a ladder from Heaven.

I do not know, or much care, whether the impulse to do all
this renovating and sandblasting was aesthetic or commercial. Bath's
best future is as a tourist town; and unlike some other tourist traps
that are bedecked and bedizened for the visitor, Bath has no need
to add anything. All it has to do to become a beautiful but animated
museum is to clean and restore and expose the lovely shell of a town
which attracted everybody there in the eighteenth century, from
Clive of India to Gainsborough, from Lady Hamilton (and Nelson,
naturally) to Sheridan and General Wolfe, Beau Nash and even John
Wesley.

The Listener
1961

JOHN BETJEMAN

The Newest Bath Guide

Proud City of Bath with your crescents and squares,
Your hoary old Abbey and playbills and chairs,
Your plentiful chapels where preachers would preach
(And a different doctrine expounded in each).
Your gallant Assemblies where squires took their daughters,
Your medicinal springs where their wives took the waters,
The comely young faces of buildings and wenches,
The cobbled back streets with their privies and stenches —
    How varied and human did Bath then appear
    As the roar of the Avon rolled up from the weir.

In those days of course there was not so much taste
But now there's so much it has all run to waste
In working out methods of cutting down cost —
So that mouldings, proportion and texture are lost
In a uniform nothingness. (This I first find
In the terrible Tech with its pointed behind).
Now houses are units, and people are digits
And Bath has been planned into quarters for midgets.
    Official designs are aggressively neuter,
    The Puritan work of an eyeless computer.

Goodbye to old Bath. We who loved you are sorry
They've carried you off by developer's lorry.

The Sack of Bath
1971

114

IAN BURTON

Another New Bath Guide

In the Assembly Room a man repairs the floor polisher.
The dawn breaks in the mirrors above the wash basins
In the Station lavatory; debtors' prison luxury.
A descendant of Lady Mary Montague's black servant
Lives in one room in Catherine Place, wets his comb,
Leans towards his chrome reflection in an Ascot heater.
Past the Church of the Nazarene, a human crocodile
From the Milbrook Training Centre, walks to the twilight
Land of the daft, to learn to bundle forewood.
Bob Steward, hair tied back, a tidy Viking,
Plays The Leaves of Life in the Ring of Bells,
Electric cables strung behind a stuffed moose head.
By the canal flight, bored boys, who don't like football,
Fish, are teased by big, blue carp.

Liberty of the Clink
1978

JAN MORRIS
The Grand Old Spa

Like Venice, Bath is rather an obfuscatory city, and it is sometimes hard to put a finger on the causes, or even the exact symptoms of this new mood. The city has always had its ups and downs. If the Romans made it one of their principal trans-Alpine resorts, the Dark Ages left it grimly derelict. If Beau Nash, the 18th-century entrepreneur, packed the nobility into its halls and salons, by the beginning of our own century the city had acquired a reputation for seedy gentility, and only a few gouty, arthritic or rheumatic familiars were to be seen taking the waters in its palm-decked Pump Room above the Roman Baths.

Vivacity does not come naturally to the place. Its setting, in a bowl in the hills above the Avon River, is picturesque but soporific. Some people suggest that the fumes of the hot springs drift invisibly about its streets, dulling all responses. The climate is nothing to write home about. Jane Austen detested the city, and the poet Alexander Pope, who often used to stay at a friend's house on the hills above, subscribed to the drifting fumes theory and thought coming downtown was like entering a sulphurous pit.

So the liveliness has to be injected, and this makes it a cyclical city, rather like a manic depressive — brilliant and abject in successive moments, or successive centuries according to the availability of talent and entreprise. Fortunately the structure of Bath as we know it today, is, by and large, the product of its heydays. The Roman remains that provide a stunning fulcrum for the town are clearly the work of a terrifically confident era — wonderful constructions, and.... all around that extraordinary core, in graceful squares and intricate pedestrian alleys, in terraces and crescents up the surrounding hills, in villas and churches and on a lovely old bridge with shops upon it, extends the Bath of the Georgian decades, the greatest single architectural monument to that age's sprightly and resilient elegance.

It is lucky for us, that Bath is so evidently entering another of its optimistic periods.... wherever you look, there seems to be initiative or restoration, and even on one of those despondent mornings when Pope's pit seems more than usually pit-like,.... somehow you feel the old place stirring with new life and bounciness.

116

Such a refulfilment will only be, after all, honoring the original destiny of the place. Even before the Romans, we are told Celts and their animals wallowed gratefully in Bath's soothing ooze and ever since visitors have managed to combine Taking the Waters with Living It Up.

As it ironically happens, the hot springs, which have been solacing people here for at least 2,000 years, have choosen this particular moment to infect themselves with a microbe, making themselves temporarily unfit for human use. Bath is in no mood, though, to be deterred by mere bugs. The little rascals, I am assured, will soon be eliminated.

The New York Times
1982

U A FANTHORPE

The West Front At Bath

The headscarfed tourists in the comfy shoes
Obediently make their scheduled pause
Among the pigeons. Sun and stone confuse
The rhythm of their uninformed applause.
Where are we now? Would it be Bath perhaps?
Five 'o' clock deftly shoots its slanted gleam
Across their eyes. A thoughtless pigeon claps
His wings. This moment is as much a dream
As Jacob's nightmare on the Abbey wall,
Alive with straining angels, who with wing
Correctly folded, desperatley crawl
Along their monstrous ladder. Evening
Distorts their poise. Above it all sits God,
Watching the dreams, and finding both kinds odd.

Side Effects
1978

SOURCES

THE RUIN - (8th-9th Century) *Codex Exoniensis*. A collection of Anglo-Saxon Poetry. It is known generally as *The Exeter Book* and contains many rare elegaic and gnomic verses of which 'The Ruin' is one. The book was bequeathed to the Library of Exeter Cathedral in 1072 by Leofric, first Bishop of Exeter. This translation of the poem (one of many) is by R.W.M. Wright and written for the 93rd Annual Meeting of the British Medical Association held at Bath in July, 1925.

THE SACRED GROVE - from *De Laudibus Divinae Sapientiae* (In Praise of Divine Wisdom) 1189. An epic poem edited and translated from the Latin by Thomas Wright in 1863. This extract is included in *The Thermal Baths of Bath* by H.W. Freeman, 1888.

IN PRAISE OF BATH - From *Libellus De Laudibus Civitatum* - Bath & Wells - by Thomas Chaundler. Translated from the original MS in the Trinity College Library by Rev. Francis Kilvert. It is described as a '...contention between the cities of Bath and Wells - a clerical dispute between one Andrew of Wells and Peter of Bath before the Bishop of Wells.

BATH - A PLEASANT BOTOM - From *The Itinerary of John Leland the Antiquary*, Part II. Published from the original MS in the Bodleian Library, by Thomas Hearne in 9 vols. (1710-1712). Leland is thought to have visited Bath between 1540 and 1542.

ADVICE ON BATHING - From *The Bathes if Bathes Ayde*, Book IV. Printed in Black Letter by William Jones of London, 1572. A rare edition of this work may be found in the Hunt Collection, Bath Ref. Library.

A TREATISE ON THE BAETH - From *A Book of the Natures and Properties - as well of the Bathes in England as of other Bathes in Germany & Italy*, by William Turner, Dean of Wells. Published by Collen, 2nd edition, 1568. This is the first known treatise which discusses the curritive properties of the natural Spas throughout Europe.

WHO MADE THE BATHS AT BATH? - From *The First Parte of the Mirour for Magistrates: Containing the Falles of the First Infortunate Princes of this Lande*. Newly corrected and Amended by Thomas Marshe: London, 1574.

BEHOLDE THE BOYLING BATHES - From *The Faerie Queen*, Book II, Canto X. Stanzas xxv, xxvi. By Edmund Spencer. This poem was written no later than 1579 and was first published in 1590.

A SONG ON THE BATHS - From *The Poetical Works of William Strode*; collected from the original MSS, 1600-1645 and printed sources. Edited by B. Dobell, London, 1907.

A SOVEREIGN CURE & A HEALTHFUL REMEDY - From *The Sonnets*, CLIII & CLIV, by William Shakespeare. London 1609. If Shakespeare visited Bath, it was as a young actor with Lord Strange's Company of Players in 1593, 1597 and 1603-4.

THE COCK-PIT CITY - Extract from a MS in the Lansdowne Collection in the BM entitled, 'A Relation of a Short Survey of Twenty-six Counties, briefly describing the Cities and their Seytuations: observ'd in a Seven Weekes Journey begun at the City of Norwich, - on Monday, August 11th, 1634 and ending in the same place. By a Captaine, a Lieutenant and an Ancient; all three of the Military Company in Norwich.

MINERVA'S SACRED SPRING - From *Poly-Olbion*, or A Chorographicall Description of the Tracts, Rivers, Mountains, Forests, and other Parts of this renowned Isle of Great Britaine, with intermixture of the most Remarquable Stories, Antiquities, Wonders, Rarityes, Pleasures and Commodities of the same. By Michael Drayton Esq. London 1613 Song III lines 194-230. Modern edition published by Oxford Shakespeare Head Press; Oxford 1933. Vol IV.

BATHONIA - From 'Philologiae, quam publice habuit ad Oxonio-Mertoneses H. Jacobius; publicavit a quin decnnio H. B (irkhead)... cum appendice luculenta. Oxon. 1652. pp 50-57.

A LETANY UPON A JOURNEY TO BATH - From *Songs and Poems of Love and Drollery* by Thomas Weaver. 1654. Ref. Pamphlets, for various verses relating to Bath. Bath Ref. Library.

A PEEP AT THE BATH - From *The Diary of Samuel Pepys* Vol. IX. 12th-15th June 1668. The original MS, now in the Pepys Library, Magdalene College, was written in shorthand covering 1660-69. It was first published in 1825 by Lord Braybooke.

A STEP TO THE BATH - With a character of the Place. From *A Step to the Bath* by Edward Ward. London 1700. Ned Ward was one of several hack writers of the period whose work featured prominently in *The London Spy*, which he edited.

THE WAYES TO THE BATH - From *Through England on a Side-Saddle in the Time of William & Mary - being the Diary of Celia Fiennes*. Published from the original MSS by Field and Tuer, London, and edited by Mrs Griffiths. Celia Fiennes journey to Bath cannot have been later than 1687.

AN INTELLIGENCE FROM THE BATH - This article first appeared in *The Guardian* No. 174, Wednesday 30th September 1713. It was later reprinted in a slim volume *The Tunbridge and Bath Miscellany for the Year 1714* by Nestor Ironside Esq. (Pseudonym for Richard Steele.)

THE PLEASURES OF THE BATH - From A Broadside entitled 'The Pleasures of the Bath: with the first and second part of the Tipling Philosophers.' Bristol: Printed by S. Farley, 1721. Another version of this popular ballad, entitled, 'The Bath Medly' with flute transposition, 1740 can be found in Vol. 3 p.177 of the Hunt Collection, Bath Ref. Library.

ON A LADY'S GOING INTO THE BATH - From *Wit and Mirth: or Pills to Purge Melancholy* - a collection of ballads and songs, by Thomas D'urfey, London, Tonson, 1719. Published in 6 vols. with songs variously set to music.

PROMISCUOUS COMPANY AT BATH - From *The Lovers Miscellancy* - or Poems on Several Occasions, Amorous and Gallant. In imitation of Mr. Prior: London 1719. The full title for this poem is, 'On the Promiscuous Mixture of Company and the Various Humours of Persons in the Hot Baths at Bath in Somersetshire'.

THE DIVERSIONS OF BATH - From *'A Tour Thro' the Whole Island of Great Britain, divided into circuits or journeys. Giving a particular & diverting account of whatever is curious and worth observation,* By a Gentleman (i.e. Daniel Defoe) 3 vols. Strahan. 1724-27. This extract is taken from Letter VI. Vol. 2. This was a popular work and after the first volume appeared in 1724 subsequently went through many editions, often enlarged and amended by other hands.

ORDERS OF HIS EXCELLENCY, R... N... Esq., Governor General of the Diversions at Bath. A facsimile and transcript of these verses which were recently discovered amongst several loose papers belonging to William Congreve, the dramatist, are with the Bath Ref. Library. The date when this poem was written is not known although Congreve did visit Bath in 1728.

THE DISEASE OF BATH - A Satire, unadorned with a frontpiece. Printed for J. Roberts at the Oxford Arms in Warwick Lane, London, 1737.

THE COMPANY AT BATH - From *A Journey through England*, In familiar letters from a Gentleman here to his friend abroad. Letter VIII Vol. 2. Caldecott, 1714.

AN EXTEMPORE, IN THE PUMP-ROOM - and dedicated to Mis H... and at Bath. 1742. From - *Miscellanies & Poems,* Vol I. by Henry Fielding Esq., printed in 3 vols. for the author by A. Millar, London. 1743.

AN EASY CURE; or a Prescription for an Invalid when at Bath. From - *The New Bath Guide,* or useful Pocket-Companion; Bath: Printed by C.Pope. price Six-pence. 1761.

A FAINT PICTURE OF BATH - From *The Life of Richard Nash, of Bath, Esq.,* Late Master of the Ceremonies at Bath, extracted principally from his original papers. London 1762 (1st & 2nd edition). Although Oliver Goldsmith wrote this work it was published anonymously.

TERRORS OF BATHING - From *The Expedition of Humphrey Clinker* by the author of Roderick Random (i.e. Tobias Smollett) 3 Vols. W. Johnson: London; B. Collins. Salisbury 1771. This extract is from Matt. Bramble's letter to Dr. Lewis, dated 28th April, Bath.

THE AMUSEMENTS OF BATH - From *An Essay Towards a Description of Bath,* Part IV Chapt. xii. (2nd edition) corrected and enlarged 2 Vols. London & Bath, 1765.

A FAREWELL TO BATH - From *The New Bath Guide: or Memoirs of the B-n-r-d Family, in a series of Poetical Epistles* by Christopher Anstey Esq., Part II Letter xv. Fletcher & Hodson, Cambridge, (2nd edition) 1766.

THE RIDOTTO OF BATH - A Panergyrick, written by a Gentleman, a resident in that City, being an Epistle from Timothy Screw under-server to Messrs Kuhf and Fitzwater, to his brother Henry, waiter at Almack's. Published originally in the Bath Chronicle, Oct. 10th 1771, it was later reprinted as a Folio Broadside and sold at a penny a copy. Richard Sheridan was just twenty years old when he wrote this piece, soon after the New Assembly Rooms were first opened.

BATH - AT THE RIGHT SEASON - From *Evelina*, or a Young Lady's Entrance into the World. - Letter XXI Vol. 3. By Francis Burney, afterwards Madame D'Arblay. Published in 3 Vols. by T. Lowndes, London 1778.

A NEW PROSE BATH GUIDE - From *The New Prose Bath Guide* for the year 1778, and printed for the author, and sold at Bath and London. This extract is from his introduction to the Guide.

A NOTE ON BATH - From *Collected Correspondence and London Notebooks of F. Joseph Haydn* - 3rd. Notebook, dated 2nd August 1794. Haydn's visit to Bath to see his friend Venanzio Rauzzini coincided with his second and last trip to England.

A RAMBLE TO BATH - From *Jacob's return from London, or his ramble to Bath*, London, J. Pitts. Broadside also Bath, W. Gye. This piece of music-hall doggeral was written and delivered by Mr. Knight, at the Theatre Royal, Bath, 1789. It was sung to the tune 'Alley Crocker'. Jacob Gawkey was a well known Somersetshire clown.

CHILDHOOD RECOLLECTIONS AT BATH - From *A Memoir of his Early Years* written by Sir Walter Scott, Ashetiel, Scotland, 26th April 1808.

SNUG LYING   From *Wonders of a Week at Bath* - "Friday" by John Cam Hobhouse otherwise known as Baron Broughton. Printed by A. Valpy, Chancery Lane, London. 1811.

A LETTER FROM BATH - From *Letters from England* by Don Manuel Alverez Espriella... translated from the Spanish. 3 Vols. 1807 Longman. This extract is from Letter LXXIV, dated Sept. 17th 1807. Published anonymously, it was however written by Robert Southey who spent a good deal of his early childhood at Bath and always retained an affection for the city.

A BRIEF SOJOURN AT BATH - From *Journal of a Tour and Residence in Great Britain* - during the years 1810-1811 by a French Traveller, Louis Simond. Vol I. (2nd edition) Edinburgh 1817.

A NEW AQUAINTANCE AT BATH - From *Northanger Abbey*, Chap. III. This was Jane Austen's first novel which she originally entitled 'Susan'. It was written in Bath about 1798/9 but wasn't published until twenty years later as a companion piece to her other novel *Persuasion* printed in 4 Vols. by John Murray, London, 1818.

APPROACH AND ARRIVAL AT BATH - From *The Invalid's and Visitor's Hand-Book to the Hot Springs of Bath* by A.B. Granville. Pub. Tilt & Bogue, London and Simms & Sons Bath, 1841. The hand-book was extracted from Granville's much larger work *Spas of England*, London 1841, Colburn 2 Vols.

AS FOR BATH - From *The Four Georges* — Sketches of Manners, Morals, Court and Town Life. by William Makepeace Thackeray, published by Smith, Elder & Co., 1861. This is a collection of essays which Thackeray wrote and delivered for his lecture tour of America. Later on he came to Bath and gave this talk on George II at the Guildhall, Bath, on January 9th 1857.

THE WATERS - From *The Posthumous Papers of the Pickwick Club*, Chapters XXXV-XXXVII. On the 31st March 1836 the first instalment of the Pickwick Papers was published in a monthly magazine The Atheneum. It consisted of twenty-six pages of text and four etchings by Robert Seymore; price 1 shilling. Charles Dickens' first recorded visit to Bath was in May 1835 working as a reporter for the Morning Chronicle.

THE TWO ERAS - or Beau Nash and the Roman. From *Sonnets, Lyrics and Translations*: Sonnet cccxix. by Charles Tennyson, afterwards Turner. London 1873.

FASHIONABLE LODGINGS - From *Miss Mackenzie* by Anthony Trollope, published by Chapman & Hall, London 1865. 2 Vols. In his autobiography Trollope claims that Mis Mackenzie was "...written with a desire to prove that a novel may be produced without any love..." Autobiography I. 10: 250.

PRIOR PARK - From *The Diary of Francis Kilvert* - 1840-1879. London. 1938-40 Jonathan Cape, 3 Vols. Chosen, introduced and edited by William Plomer. Born near Bath in 1793 and educated at King Edward's School, Bath, Kilvert became the curate of Claverton. He wrote many papers on the history of Bath for the Bath Literary Society. He was also the City's tax and rate collector.

A TRUE BLOT IN BATH - From *Far From the Madding Crowd* - Chapter XXXIII - entitled A Harbinger. First published by Smith, Elder & Co., 2 Vols. 1874.

A BALLAD OF BATH - From - *Poems and Ballads* - 3rd series. by A.C. Swinburne. London 1901.

THE KING OF BATH - From *Monsieur Beaucaire* - A Tale. published by John Murray, London 1901. This amusing story set in the hey-day of Beau Nash was produced at the Comedy Theatre, London on 7th Feb. 1903 and later made into a feature film starring Bob Hope as Monsieur Beaucaire.

QUEEN BATH - From *The Day and other Poems* by Henry Chappell, otherwise known as the Porter Poet who worked for British Railways at Bath Spa Station. London, Bodley Head, 1918.

AQUAE SULIS - From *Satires and Circumstance. Lyrics and Reveries etc.*, London, 1914. A signed copy of this poem (four stanzas only) written in Hardy's own hand and dated 1912 is in the posession of Bath Ref. Library.

ON BATH - From *Generally Speaking*, Chapter XXI. This collection of essays was originally published in The Illustrated London News. London, Methuen & Co., 1928.

I SINK INTO BATH - From *In Search of England*, Chapter VI. First published by Methuen, London, 1927. This popular work has since gone through many editions since it first appeared.

BATH BY MOONLIGHT - From 'Secret Places of the Heart' published by Hutchinson & co., London 1933. This is one of three stories by H.G. Wells which he included in a volume entitled *Stories of Men and Women in Love*, published by Hutchinson & Co., London, 1933. In 1922 Wells, a sick man at the time, visited Bath and stayed at the Pulteney Hotel at the same time that he was writing this story.

BATH, PAST AND PRESENT - From 'On Tour in England, Bath, Bristol and Cheltenham' published under the title *On the Move in England* by Hutchinson & Co., London, 1940. This extract first appeared as an article in *The Sunday Times*, 26th February 1939 and was the first in a series written by the celebrated cartoonist H.M. Bateman.

ELEVENES - From *Punch*, September 10th 1941 p.230

THE BOMBED CITY - From *In Yeovil Town* - Poems by Charles Whitby, published by the Fortune Press, London, 1947. This poem is the third in a sonnet sequence entitled Bath in Wartime for the periods 1939, 1941 and 1942.

BATH - From *Poetry Quarterly* Vol. 7. No. 3. by Wrenne Jarman, published only in this issue 1945.

A LETTER FROM BATH - Alistair Cooke reflects on the City and Frank Lloyd Wright. This article was printed in *The Listener* dated 6th July 1961.

THE NEWEST BATH GUIDE - From *The Sack of Bath* - by Adam Fergusson, published by Compton Russell, 1973. The poem 'In a Bath Tea Shop' has of course immortalised J.B. Priestly's link with this city.

ANOTHER BATH GUIDE - From *Liberty of the Clink* a collection of poems by Bath's resident and finest poets, Ian Burton. Published by Paris Garden Press, 1977.

THE GRAND OLD SPA OF BATH RECAPTURES ITS HIGH SPIRITS From an article by Jan Morris published in *The New York Times*, Sunday 28th March, 1982. Jan Morris was for some years a resident of Bath City.

THE WEST FRONT AT BATH - From *Side Effects* by U.A. Fanthorpe. Published by Harry Chambers/Peterloo Poets, 1978.

FURTHER READING

BETJEMAN, John: *Collected Poems*, John Murray, London, 1980

BOOTH, Stephen: *Shakespeare's Sonnets* with analytic commentary. Yale University Press, 1977

CHANDLER, Mary: *A Description of Bath - A Poem*, Humbly inscribed to H.R.H. Princess Amelia, London & Bath 1734 for J. Leake

D'URFEY, Thomas: *The Bath or The Western Lass* - A Comedy as it is Acted at the Theatre Royal, Drury Lane, London 1701

DERRY, Warren: *Journals and Letters of Fanny Burney*, Oxford, Clarendon Press, 1972

GRANVILLE, Augustus Bozzi: *Spas of England*, London, Colburn 1841

GREENLAW, E: *The Works of Edmund Spencer*, a Variorum Edition, John Hopkins Press, Baltimore, USA, 1933

GRIFFITHS, Mrs: *Through England on a Side-Saddle*, London, Field & Tuer, 1888

HUMPHRIES, Lund: *Exeter Book of Old English Poetry*, 1933

JAMES, Montague Rhodes, editor: *The Chaundler MSS*, printed for the Roxburghe Club, 1916

LATHAM, Robert & MATHEWS, W: *The Diary of Samuel Pepys*, London, G. Bell & Sons Ltd, 1976

LEVIS, H.C: *The British King Who Tried to Fly*, Cheswick Press, London, 1919

LOCKHART, J.G: *Narrative of the Life of Sir Walter Scott*, begun by Himself and continued by Lockhart, 2 Vols, R. Codell, Edinburgh, 1848

PRIOR, Mathew: *Poems on Several Occasions, Amorous and Gallant*, Tonson, 1709

ROBERTSON, Charles: *Bath, An Architectural Guide*, London, Faber & Faber, 1975

ROBBINS LANDON, H.C: *Collected Correspondences and London Notebooks of Joseph Haydn*, London, Barrie & Rockliff, 1959

WHITBY, Charles: *The Bath Anthology*, London, Folk Press, 1928

WOOD, John: *Essay Towards a Description of Bath*, Facsimile of 2nd. edition, Bath, Kingsmead Reprints, 1969

WRIGHT, Reginald W.M: written for the 93rd. Annual Meeting of the British Medical Association, held at Bath, July 1925. Bound under the title *The Book of Bath*, 1925

INDEX OF AUTHORS